Pocket
ROME
TOP SIGHTS • LOCAL LIFE • MADE EASY

Duncan Garwood

In This Book

QuickStart Guide

Your keys to understanding the city – we help you decide what to do and how to do it

Need to Know
Tips for a smooth trip

Neighbourhoods
What's where

Explore Rome

The best things to see and do, neighbourhood by neighbourhood

Top Sights
Make the most of your visit

Local Life
The insider's city

The Best of Rome

The city's highlights in handy lists to help you plan

Best Walks
See the city on foot

Rome's Best...
The best experiences

Survival Guide

Tips and tricks for a seamless, hassle-free city experience

Getting Around
Travel like a local

Essential Information
Including where to stay

Our selection of the city's best places to eat, drink and experience:

◉ **Sights**

✖ **Eating**

🍷 **Drinking**

✪ **Entertainment**

🔒 **Shopping**

These symbols give you the vital information for each listing:

🕿 Telephone Numbers	👫 Family-Friendly
🕑 Opening Hours	🐾 Pet-Friendly
🅿 Parking	🚌 Bus
🚭 Nonsmoking	⛴ Ferry
@ Internet Access	Ⓜ Metro
🛜 Wi-Fi Access	Ⓢ Subway
🥗 Vegetarian Selection	🚃 Tram
📖 English-Language Menu	🚆 Train

Find each listing quickly on maps for each neighbourhood:

Bar Hemingway

16 🍷 Map p233, B2

Legend has it that Hemi self, wielding a machine rate this timber-pan ered bar during showpiece is a en by Papa ar town. Dress s.com; Hôtel Rit ⊙6.30pm-2a

6 ◉ Plac

Lonely Planet's Rome

Lonely Planet Pocket Guides are designed to get you straight to the heart of the city.

Inside you'll find all the must-see sights, plus tips to make your visit to each one really memorable. We've split the city into easy-to-navigate neighbourhoods and provided clear maps so you'll find your way around with ease. Our expert authors have searched out the best of the city: walks, food, nightlife and shopping, to name a few. Because you want to explore, our 'Local Life' pages will take you to some of the most exciting areas to experience the real Rome.

And of course you'll find all the practical tips you need for a smooth trip: itineraries for short visits, how to get around, and how much to tip the guy who serves you a drink at the end of a long day's exploration.

It's your guarantee of a really great experience.

Our Promise

You can trust our travel information because Lonely Planet authors visit the places we write about, each and every edition. We never accept freebies for positive coverage, so you can rely on us to tell it like it is.

QuickStart Guide 7

Explore Rome 21

Worth a Trip:

The Best of Rome 165

Rome's Best Walks

Rome's Best...

Survival Guide 189

QuickStart Guide

Welcome to Rome

An epic, monumental city, Rome gets under your skin fast. Even on a short break, you'll be smitten by its artistic masterpieces and iconic monuments, operatic piazzas and haunting ruins. Life is lived to the full here, and the city teems with trattorias and designer restaurants, street-side bars and glam fashion boutiques. Visit once and you'll be hooked for life.

St Peter's Basilica (p138)
WILL SALTER/LONELY PLANET IMAGES ©

Rome
Top Sights

Colosseum (p24)

Rome's most iconic monument, the Colosseo is an electrifying sight. An architectural tour de force, it has been drawing the crowds since it first staged gladiatorial combat in the 1st century AD.

Vatican Museums (p142)

The colossal Musei Vaticani complex boasts some of the world's most celebrated works of art, including Michelangelo's frescoes in the Sistine Chapel (Cappella Sistina) and Raphael's masterpiece *La scuola di Atene* (The School of Athens).

Museo e Galleria Borghese (p156)

Home to the 'queen of all private art collections', this magnificent gallery showcases the best of Bernini's baroque sculpture, as well as works by Canova, Caravaggio, Raphael and Titian.

Pantheon (p38)

The best preserved of Rome's ancient monuments, this is one of the world's most influential buildings. Its design and record-breaking dome have inspired architects for centuries, and it remains a thrilling sight.

Museo Nazionale Romano: Palazzo Massimo alle Terme (p80)

Housed in a Renaissance palace near the bus station, this is one of Rome's less-heralded highlights, harbouring heavyweight classical sculpture and some impressive ancient mosaics.

Appian Way (p104)

Flanked by green fields and umbrella pine trees, Via Appia Antica, the queen of ancient roads, has a morbid history – Spartacus was crucified here and the early Christians buried their dead in the catacombs.

Roman Forum (p26)

Walk in the footsteps of Julius Caesar and the great rulers of Roman history as you explore the tumbledown ruins of the Foro Romano, once the glittering heart of the Roman Empire.

Spanish Steps & Piazza di Spagna (p56)

The Scalinata di Trinità dei Monti have provided a perch for tourists and poseurs since the 18th century. There are memorable rooftop views from the top and a circus-like atmosphere on the piazza below.

Basilica di San Giovanni in Laterano (p96)

A striking display of baroque bombast, this landmark basilica is the city's oldest, dating to the dog days of the Roman Empire.

Basilica di Santa Maria in Trastevere (p122)

Discreetly tucked away on a charming piazza, this low-key looker was built on the site where an ancient miracle took place, and features some extraordinary 12th-century mosaics.

GEOFF STRINGER/LONELY PLANET IMAGES ©

WIBOWO RUSLI/LONELY PLANET IMAGES ©

St Peter's Basilica (p138)

A monument to artistic genius, the Basilica di San Pietro is Rome's largest and most spectacular church, the most important in the Catholic world. Behind the grandiose facade, priceless artworks litter its lavish interior.

Trevi Fountain (p68)

A favourite film backdrop, Rome's most celebrated fountain is a gloriously over-the-top affair. Visitors flock to the Fontana di Trevi to toss a coin into the water and ensure their return to Rome.

Rome
Local Life

Insider tips to help you find the real city

It's easy to be blinded by Rome's beauty, but scratch beneath the surface and you'll discover another side to the city. Here we explore the city's alternative hang-outs and boho bar haunts, its hot clubs and off-the-radar neighbourhoods.

A Day Out in the Centro Storico (p40)

▶ Beautiful backdrops
▶ Spa and shopping

Once you've covered the Pantheon, Piazza Navona and the centre's big headline sights, it's time to slow down and enjoy the area like the locals do – catch an exhibition, shop for jeans, soak in a spa and dine on pizza and beer. All against the most beautiful of backdrops.

San Lorenzo & Il Pigneto (p92)

▶ Bohemian bars
▶ Alternative art

Head to graffiti-clad San Lorenzo and boho Pigneto to admire one of Rome's major basilicas,

catch some contemporary art and revel in laid-back nightlife. You can join fashion-conscious diners at smart restaurants and drink with students at grungy bars.

Ostiense & San Paolo (p118)

▶ Cool clubs
▶ Hidden culture

With its disused factories, authentic trattorias and university campus, Ostiense is home to Rome's hottest clubs and hippest bars. But before the nightlife revs up, you can explore several fascinating cultural gems, including Rome's second-largest basilica, an ex–power station turned art gallery, and the

unique Garbatella neighbourhood.

A Night Out in Trastevere (p124)

▶ Heaving bars
▶ Aperitif and pizza

A picturesque district full of bars, cafes and trattorias, Trastevere has long been a foreigner favourite. But Romans love it, too, and amid the tourist bustle you'll find some characteristic city haunts. Come in the early evening for an aperitif, followed by dinner and cool tunes.

Statue in the Centrale Montemartini (p119), Ostiense

Piazza Santa Maria in Trastevere (p125)

Other great places to experience the city like a local:

Jewish Ghetto (p48)

Via Margutta (p59)

Auditorium Parco della Musica (p163)

Via del Boschetto (p91)

Piazza del Quirinale (p71)

Monte Testaccio (p113)

Pasticceria Regoli (p88)

Trastevere, Festa di Noantri (p130)

Pastificio (p62)

Rome
Day Planner

Day One

With only one day, follow this tour through the city's ancient wonders. Start at the **Colosseum** (p24) – get there early to avoid the worst queues. Then head on to the **Palatino** (p31) to poke around crumbling ruins and admire sweeping views. From the Palatino follow the path down into the **Roman Forum** (p26), an evocative area of tumbledown temples and sprouting columns. Done there, finish your trawl through the city's great ruins at the **Mercati di Traiano Museo dei Fori Imperiali** (p32).

After lunch at the **Enoteca Provincia Romana** (p33), climb the Cordonata to **Piazza del Campidoglio** (p31) and the **Capitoline Museums** (p31). Here you'll find some stunning ancient sculpture and paintings by a selection of big-name artists. To clear your head afterwards, pop in to **Il Vittoriano** (p31) and take the lift to the top for Rome's best 360-degree views.

Spend the evening in the *centro storico* (historic centre). Dine on authentic Roman cuisine at **Armando al Pantheon** (p47) before rounding off the day with a cocktail at **Salotto 42** (p51).

Day Two

On day two, hit the Vatican. First up, grab a *cornetto* (Italian croissant) from **Dolce Maniera** (p152), then plunge into the **Vatican Museums** (p142). Once you've blown your mind on the Sistine Chapel and the other highlights, continue to **St Peter's Basilica** (p138). Afterwards, grab a slice of gourmet pizza at **Pizzarium** (p150) or a slap-up trattoria meal at **Hostaria Dino & Tony** (p151).

Recharged, stop off at **Castel Sant'Angelo** (p150), Rome's landmark castle, en route to the *centro storico*. Here you'll come across some of the city's great sights, including **Piazza Navona** (p44) and the **Pantheon** (p38). Art lovers can admire paintings by Caravaggio in the **Chiesa di San Luigi dei Francesi** (p44) and fashionistas can browse the boutiques on Via del Governo Vecchio.

After a romantic dinner at **Casa Coppelle** (p47), stop in the centre for a taste of *dolce vita* bar life. Depending on what you're after, you could hang out with the beautiful people at **Etablì** (p51), sup beer at **Open Baladin** (p41) or chat over coffee at **Caffè Sant'Eustachio** (p50).

Short on time?
We've arranged Rome's must-sees into these day-by-day itineraries to make sure you see the very best of the city in the time you have available.

Day Three

☀ Day three starts with a trip to the **Museo e Galleria Borghese** (p156) to marvel at amazing baroque sculpture. Afterwards, stroll through **Villa Borghese** (p160) down to the **Galleria Nazionale d'Arte Moderna** (p160) for an injection of modern art. Lunch at the gallery's elegant cafe, the **Caffè delle Arti** (p162).

☀ In the afternoon, check out **Piazza del Popolo** (p59) and then investigate the area around **Piazza di Spagna** (p56). Plan your moves while sitting on the **Spanish Steps** and then dive down Via dei Condotti to shop at the flagship designer stores. From Via del Corso, at the bottom, make your way to the **Trevi Fountain** (p68), where tradition dictates you throw a coin in to ensure your return to Rome.

☾ Over the river, the picture-perfect Trastevere neighbourhood bursts with life in the evening as locals and tourists flock to its many eateries and bars. Get into the mood with an aperitif at **Freni e Frizioni** (p125) before pizza at **Dar Poeta** (p131) or a refined dinner at **Glass Hostaria** (p130).

Day Four

☀ On day four it's time to venture out to the **Appian Way** (p104) and the wonderfully creepy catacombs. Above ground, you'll find the remains of an ancient racetrack in the grounds of the **Villa di Massenzio** (p105). For lunch, head back into town to the highly regarded **Trattoria Monti** (p86).

☀ Start the afternoon by visiting the **Museo Nazionale Romano: Palazzo Massimo alle Terme** (p80), a really superb museum full of classical sculpture and stunning mosaics. Then, drop by the monumental **Basilica di Santa Maria Maggiore** (p84), famous for its mosaics, and the **Basilica di San Pietro in Vincoli** (p84), home to Michelangelo's muscular *Moses* sculpture. Continue on down to the charming Monti district for some fashionable shopping.

☾ Stay put in Monti, where there's plenty of late-night action. Dine on meaty Umbrian fare at the excellent **L'Asino d'Oro** (p87) and then take your pick of wine bar or cafe to see out the day. **Ai Tre Scalini** (p88) is a popular local choice.

Need to Know

For more information, see Survival Guide (p189).

Currency
Euro (€)

Language
Italian

Visas
Not required by EU citizens. Not required by nationals of Australia, Canada, New Zealand and the USA for stays of up to 90 days.

Money
ATMs are widespread. Major credit cards are widely accepted but some smaller shops and trattorias may not take them. Keep cash for immediate expenses.

Mobile Phones
Local SIM cards can be used in European, Australian and unlocked US phones. Other phones must be set to roaming.

Time
Western European Time (GMT/UTC plus one hour)

Plugs & Adaptors
Plugs have two or three round pins; electricity is 220V to 230V; North American travellers will require an adaptor and transformer.

Tipping
Not obligatory, but round up the bill in pizzerias or leave about 5%; 10% is normal in upmarket restaurants.

1 Before You Go

Your Daily Budget

Budget under €70
▶ Dorm bed €15–35
▶ Pizza meal plus beer €15
▶ Drink coffee standing at the bar
▶ Eat with an *aperitivo* to save money

Midrange €70–200
▶ Double room €120–250
▶ Three-course restaurant meal €30–50
▶ B&Bs are often better value than hotels

Top End over €200
▶ Double room €250 plus
▶ City taxi ride €5–15
▶ Auditorium concert tickets €25–90

Useful Websites

Lonely Planet (www.lonelyplanet.com/rome) Planning info, hotels and traveller forum.

060608 (www.060608.it) City tourist site.

Coop Culture (www.coopculture.it) Information and ticket booking for Rome's monuments.

Vatican (www.vatican.va) Book tickets for the Vatican Museums.

Advance Planning

Two months before Book high-season rooms.

One to two weeks before Reserve tables at A-list restaurants. Sort out tickets to the pope's weekly audience at the Vatican.

A few days before Phone for tickets for the Museo e Galleria Borghese and book for the Vatican Museums.

② Arriving in Rome

Most visitors arrive at one of Rome's two airports: Leonardo da Vinci, also known as Fiumicino; or Ciampino, hub for European low-cost carrier Ryanair – see www.adr.it. International trains serve Stazione Termini in the city centre.

✈ From Aeroporto Internazionale Leonardo da Vinci (Fiumicino)

Destination	Best Transport
Monti & Esquilino	Leonardo Express train, then metro line A or B
Centro Storico	Leonardo Express train, then bus
Trastevere	FR1 train, then tram 8
Vatican	Leonardo Express train, then metro line A
Tridente	Leonardo Express train, then metro line A

✈ From Aeroporto di Roma Ciampino

Destination	Best Transport
Monti & Esquilino	Terravision/SIT bus, then metro line A or B
Centro Storico	Terravision/SIT bus, then bus
Trastevere	Terravision/SIT bus, then bus
Vatican	Terravision/SIT bus, then metro line A
Tridente	Terravision/SIT bus, then metro line A

🚌 From Stazione Termini

Airport buses and trains, and international trains, arrive at Stazione Termini. From here you can take metro line A or B or hop on a bus to all main neighbourhoods. Taxis are available outside the main entrance.

③ Getting Around

Public transport is cheap and reasonably efficient, although strikes, which are not uncommon, can cause chaos. Buy a one- or three-day pass to save time and money. For information and a route planner, see www.atac.roma.it.

Ⓜ Metro

The metro is the quickest way of getting around central Rome, although it's of limited use for the *centro storico* (historic centre). Lines A (orange) and B (blue) cross the city in an X-shape, crossing at Stazione Termini. Services run from 5.30am to 11.30pm (to 1.30am on Friday and Saturday).

🚌 Bus

Chaotic traffic can slow buses, but they are still the best bet for the *centro storico*. Most routes pass by Stazione Termini. Buses run from 5.30am until midnight, with limited services throughout the night. Remember to validate tickets in the yellow machines on board.

🚋 Tram

Tram 8 is the most useful, connecting the centre with Trastevere over the river. Trams are also useful for San Lorenzo and Il Pigneto.

🚕 Taxi

Taxis are useful late at night when bus services are slow and the metro has closed. Pick them up at a taxi rank or phone for one – try **taxi line** (📞06 06 09). Surcharges apply after 10pm and for carrying luggage.

Rome
Neighbourhoods

Tridente (p54)
Designer stores and swank bars set the tone for this stylish, upmarket district centred on two striking piazzas.

⊙ **Top Sights**
Spanish Steps & Piazza di Spagna

Vatican City & Prati (p136)
Feast on extravagant art in the monumental Vatican and excellent food in neighbouring Prati.

⊙ **Top Sights**
St Peter's Basilica
Vatican Museums

Centro Storico (p36)
Rome's historic centre is the capital's thumping heart – a heady warren of famous squares and tangled lanes, galleries, restaurants and bars.

⊙ **Top Sights**
Pantheon

Trastevere & Gianicolo (p120)
Trastevere's medieval streets heave with kicking bars and eateries. The Gianicolo offers to-die-for panoramas.

⊙ **Top Sights**
Basilica di Santa Maria in Trastevere

Ancient Rome (p22)
Rome's ancient core is a beautiful area of evocative ruins, improbable legends, soaring pine trees and panoramic views.

⊙ **Top Sights**
Colosseum
Roman Forum

Vatican Museums ⊙

St Peter's Basilica

Spanish Steps & Piazza di Spagna ⊙

Pantheon ⊙

Trevi Fountain ⊙

Basilica di Santa Maria in Trastevere ⊙

Roman Forum ⊙

Villa Borghese & Around (p154)
Dominated by Villa Borghese park, this moneyed area has some superb cultural offerings, including one of Rome's top galleries.

⊙ **Top Sights**
Museo e Galleria Borghese

Trevi & the Quirinale (p66)
A busy, hilly district, home to Rome's most famous fountain, Italy's presidential palace and several stellar art galleries.

⊙ **Top Sights**
Trevi Fountain

Monti & Esquilino (p78)
Boutiques and wine bars abound in Monti, while Esquilino offers multiculturalism and several must-see museums and churches.

⊙ **Top Sights**
Museo Nazionale Romano: Palazzo Massimo alle Terme

⊙ *Museo e Galleria Borghese*

⊙ *Museo Nazionale Romano: Palazzo Massimo alle Terme*

⊙ *Colosseum*

⊙ *Basilica di San Giovanni in Laterano*

Celio & Lateran (p94)
Explore medieval churches and escape the tourist crowds in the leafy Celio and residential San Giovanni districts.

⊙ **Top Sights**
Basilica di San Giovanni in Laterano

Aventino & Testaccio (p108)
Ideal for a romantic getaway, hilltop Aventino rises above Testaccio, famous for its nose-to-tail cooking and thumping nightlife.

⊙ *Appian Way*

Worth a Trip
⊙ **Top Sights**
Appian Way

Explore
Rome

Ponte Sant'Angelo leading to Castel Sant'Angelo (p150)
RICHARD I'ANSON/LONELY PLANET IMAGES ©

Explore

Ancient Rome

In a city of extraordinary beauty, Rome's ancient heart stands out. It's here that you'll find the great icons of the city's past: the Colosseum, the Palatino, the Roman and Imperial Forums, and Piazza del Campidoglio, home to the mighty Capitoline Museums. Touristy by day, the area is quiet at night, with few after-hours attractions.

The Sights in a Day

☀ Start early at the **Colosseum** (p24), Rome's fearsome gladiatorial arena. From there, continue on to the **Palatino** (p31) to see where Romulus supposedly founded the city. Before leaving the area take a moment to look down onto the **Roman Forum** (p26), your next destination. Once you've explored the ruins, exit the forum and climb up to **Piazza del Campidoglio** (p31) and the hilltop **Chiesa di Santa Maria in Aracoeli** (p31). Round the morning off with a doorstopper panino from **Alimentari Pannella Carmela** (p35).

☀ After lunch, it's time for the **Capitoline Museums** (p31) and their collection of sculpture and major paintings. To clear your head afterwards, pop in to **Il Vittoriano** (p31) and take the lift to the top for Rome's best 360-degree views. If you've got energy for one last museum, the **Mercati di Traiano Museo dei Fori Imperiali** (p32) provides a thrilling overview of the Imperial Forums.

☾ Finish the day with dinner and excellent local wine at the **Enoteca Provincia Romana** (p33) overlooking the Colonna di Traiano (Trajan's Column).

 Top Sights

Colosseum (p24)

Roman Forum (p26)

 Best of Rome

History
Colosseum (p24)

Roman Forum (p26)

Palatino (p31)

Bocca della Verità (p33)

Architecture
Colosseum (p24)

Mercati di Traiano Museo dei Fori Imperiali (p32)

Piazza del Campidoglio (p31)

Getting There

Ⓜ **Metro** The best option for the Colosseum, Roman and Imperial Forums and Palatino is metro line B to Colosseo – at Termini follow signs for line B *direzione* (towards) Laurentina.

Ⓜ **Metro** Another useful stop on line B is Circo Massimo, just southeast of the site of the same name.

🚌 **Bus** Frequent buses head to Piazza Venezia, including buses 40, 64, 87, 170, 916 and H.

Top Sights
Colosseum

Originally known as the Flavian Amphitheatre, the 50,000-seat Colosseum (Colosseo) is the most thrilling of Rome's ancient sights. It was here that gladiators met in mortal combat and where condemned prisoners fought wild beasts in front of baying, bloodthirsty crowds. Inaugurated in AD 80, it fell into disrepair after the fall of the Roman Empire, and was later used as a quarry for travertine and marble.

⊙ Map p30, D4

www.pierreci.it

Piazza del Colosseo

adult/reduced incl Roman Forum & Palatino €12/7.50

🕑8.30am-1hr before sunset

Ⓜ Colosseo

Don't Miss

The Exterior
The outer walls, which were originally covered in travertine, have three levels of arches, articulated by Ionic, Doric and Corinthian columns. The entrance arches, known as *vomitoria*, allowed the spectators to enter and be seated in minutes, whilst up top, the upper level had supports for 240 masts that held up a canvas awning over the arena.

The Arena
The arena had a wooden floor covered in sand to prevent the combatants from slipping and to soak up the blood. It could also be flooded for mock sea battles. Trapdoors led down to the hypogeum, an underground complex of corridors, cages and lifts that served as the stadium's back-stage area.

Seating
The *cavea*, for spectator seating, was divided into three tiers: magistrates and senior officials sat in the lowest tier, wealthy citizens in the middle and the plebs in the highest tier. Women (except for vestal virgins) were relegated to the cheapest sections at the top. The podium, a broad terrace in front of the tiers of seats, was reserved for emperors, senators and VIPs.

Arco di Costantino
Although not part of the Colosseum, the Arco di Costantino (Arch of Constantine) is a handsome landmark. Built in 312, it commemorates Constantine's victory over his rival Maxentius at the Battle of Ponte Milvio.

☑ Top Tips

▶ Visit in the early morning or late afternoon to avoid the crowds.

▶ If queues are long, buy your ticket at the Palatino or Roman Forum.

▶ Other queue-jumping tips: get the **Roma Pass** (www.romapass.it); book your ticket online at www.pierreci.it; or join an official English-language tour (€5 on top of the regular ticket).

▶ If you have your photo taken with a costumed centurion, they'll expect a tip – no more than €5.

✕ Take a Break

Avoid the rip-off food trucks outside the arena. Instead, head up to Cavour 313 (p35) for a light meal and glass of wine. On the Circo Massimo, and a bit of a walk from the Colosseum, 0,75 (p35) is a good bet for a lunchtime pasta or relaxed drink.

Top Sights
Roman Forum

The Roman Forum (Foro Romano) was ancient Rome's showpiece centre, a grandiose district of marble-clad temples, basilicas and vibrant public spaces. Its impressive, but badly labelled, ruins give some hint of this but you'll still have to use your imagination to picture it as it once was. Dating to the 7th century BC when it was first developed as an Etruscan burial ground, it fell into disrepair after the fall of the Roman Empire.

👁 Map p30, B3

www.pierreci.it

Largo della Salara Vecchia

adult/reduced incl Colosseum & Palatino €12/7.50

🕗8.30am-1hr before sunset

Ⓜ Colosseo

Don't Miss

Via Sacra

Via Sacra, the Forum's main thoroughfare, connected the Palatino with the Roman Forum and Campidoglio. Lined with basilicas and temples – the **Basilica Fulvia Aemilia**, the **Tempio di Romolo** and the **Tempio di Antonino e Faustina** – it was part of the route that military commanders followed during the Roman Triumph, a ceremonial procession staged to honour their victories.

Curia

This big barn-like building was the official seat of the Roman Senate. Little remains of the 44 BC original and most of what you see today is a reconstruction of the Curia as it looked in the 3rd-century reign of Diocletian. In front, and hidden by scaffolding, is the **Lapis Niger**, a piece of black marble that covers the tomb of Romulus.

Rostrum & Colonna di Foca

Marking the centre of Piazza del Foro, the forum's main square, is the Colonna di Foca (Column of Phocus), a free-standing, 13.5m-high column dating to AD 608. Behind it are the remains of the Rostrum, an elaborate podium where Shakespeare had Mark Antony make his famous 'Friends, Romans, countrymen...' speech, and local politicos would harangue the market crowds.

Arco di Settimio Severo

One of the Roman Forum's signature monuments, and one of the finest examples of its type in Italy, the imposing 23m-high Arch of Septimius Severus was built in AD 203 to celebrate Roman victories over the Parthians. If you can make them out, reliefs in the central panel depict the defeated Parthians being led away in chains.

☑ Top Tips

▶ Get grandstand views of the Roman Forum from the Palatino and Campidoglio.

▶ Visit early morning or late afternoon; crowds are worst between 11am and 2pm.

▶ It can get very hot and there's little shade, so take a hat and plenty of water.

▶ If you're caught short, there are toilets near the Tempio di Castore e Polluce.

✗ Take a Break

For a restorative coffee break head up to the Campidoglio and the Caffè Capitolino (p35). If you need something more substantial, search out the Enoteca Provincia Romana (p33), which serves high-quality regional food.

Tempio di Saturno

The eight granite columns that rise up behind the Colonna are all that remain of the Temple of Saturn, an important temple that doubled as the state treasury. Behind it (from north to south) are the ruins of the **Tempio della Concordia** (Temple of Concord), the **Tempio di Vespasiano** (Temple of Vespasian and Titus) and the **Portico degli Dei Consenti**.

Tempio di Castore e Polluce

Only three Corinthian columns remain of the Temple of Castor and Pollux, also known as the Tempio dei Castori. The temple, which dates to 489 BC, was dedicated to the Heavenly Twins after they supposedly led the Romans to victory over the Etruscan Tarquins.

Tempio di Giulio Cesare

Little now remains of the Temple of Julius Caesar, aka the Tempio del Divo Giulio, erected by Augustus in 29 BC on the site where Caesar's body had been cremated 15 years earlier. Caesar was the first Roman to be posthumously deified, a custom that was central to the Roman imperial cult.

Casa delle Vestali

White statues line the grassy atrium of the House of the Vestal Virgins, the once-luxurious, 50-room home of the virgins who tended the flame in the adjoining **Tempio di Vesta** (Temple of Vesta, goddess of hearth and household).

Basilica di Massenzio

Started by Emperor Maxentius and finished by Constantine (it's also known as the Basilica di Costantino) in 315, this vast basilica, the largest on the forum, covered an area of approximately 100m by 65m. In its original form the central hall was divided into enormous naves but only part of the northern nave survives to this day.

Arco di Tito

Said to be the inspiration for the Arc de Triomphe in Paris, the well-preserved Arch of Titus was built in AD 81 to celebrate Vespasian's and Titus' victories against Jewish rebels in Jerusalem. In the past, Roman Jews would avoid passing under the arch, the historical symbol of the beginning of the Diaspora.

Understand
The Vestal Virgins

Despite privilege and public acclaim, life as a vestal virgin was no bed of roses. Every year six physically perfect patrician girls between the ages of six and 10 were chosen by lottery to serve in the Tempio di Vesta for a period of 30 years. If they lost their virginity they risked being buried alive and their lover being flogged to death.

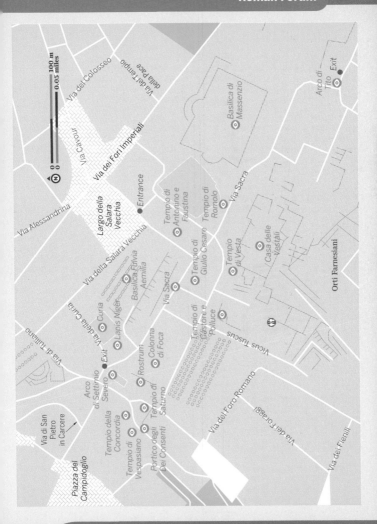

100 m
0.05 miles

Via del Colosseo
Via del Tempio della Pace
Via Cavour
Via dei Fori Imperiali
Arco di Tito · Exit
Basilica di Massenzio
Via Sacra
Via Alessandrina
Entrance
Largo della Salara Vecchia
Tempio di Antonino e Faustina
Tempio di Romolo
Via della Salara Vecchia
Basilica Fulvia Aemilia
Tempio di Giulio Cesare
Tempio di Vesta
Casa delle Vestali
Orti Farnesiani
Curia
Lapis Niger
Via della Curia
Via Sacra
Via di Tulliano
Exit
Rostrum
Colonna di Foca
Tempio di Castore e Polluce
Vicus Tuscus
Arco di Settimio Severo
Via di San Pietro in Carcere
Tempio della Concordia
Tempio di Vespasiano
Tempio di Saturno
Portico degli Dei Consenti
Via del Foro Romano
Via dei Fienili
Piazza del Campidoglio
Via dei Foraggi

A

Piazza
8 Venezia
Via IV Novembre
Museo Nazionale
del Palazzo Venezia 10
Piazza
di San Marco
Via di
San Marco
5
Il Vittoriano
Piazza
d'Ara
Coeli
Via
d'Aracoeli
4 Chiesa di Santa
Maria in Aracoeli
Capitoline
Museums
3 2
14
Via di
Monte
Caprino
Via Consolazione
11
12

B

Mercati di Traiano
Museo dei Fori Imperiali
6
Colonna di
Traiano
Imperial
Forums
7
Via dei Fori Imperiali
Via Alessandrina
Piazza del Campidoglio
Largo
della Salara
Vecchia
Via dei Foraggi

C

Via Nazionale
Largo
Angelicum
Via Baccina
Via Tor de' Conti
Via della Madonna de' Monti 13
Largo C Ricci
Via del Colosseo

D

Via Panisperna
Via Cimarra
Piazza
Madonn
dei Mon
Piazza Sa
Francesc
di Paola
Via Cavour
Via Frangipane

N 0   200 m
  0   0.1 miles

Roman Forum

Via dei Fori Imperiali

Largo G
Agnesi

Via N Salvi

Colosseo

Orti Farnesiani

Piazza
di Santa
Maria Nova
Via Sacra

Colosseum

Arco di Costantino

Piazza del
Colosseo

Vigna
Barberini

Via di San Teodoro

Via Petroselli

Via del Velabro

Via di San Gregorio

Via Celio Vibenna

CAMPITELLI

Bocca
9 della
Verità

Via della
Greca

Via d'Ara
Mass di Ercole

Clivio dei Publicii

Piazza di
Sant'Anastasia

Via del Cerchio

15

1
Palatino

Viale del Parco del Celio

Clivo di Scauro

Parco
Savello

Via del Circo
Massimo

Circo
Massimo

For reviews see	
Top Sights	p24
Sights	p31
Eating	p33
Drinking	p35

Sights

Palatino
ANCIENT RUINS

1 ◉ Map p30, C5

The Palatino (Palatine), ancient Rome's smartest neighbourhood, is steeped in myth. It was here that Romulus supposedly founded the city in 753 BC and Rome's emperors lived in unabashed luxury. Highlights include the ruins of the main imperial palace and the archaeological artefacts of the Museo Palatino. For grandstand views over the Roman Forum, head to the Orti Farnesiani. (www.pierreci.it; Via di San Gregorio 30; adult/reduced incl Colosseum & Roman Forum €12/7.50; ⏰8.30am-1hr before sunset; Ⓜ Colosseo)

Piazza del Campidoglio
PIAZZA

2 ◉ Map p30, A2

Climb the **Cordonata**, the graceful staircase that leads up from Piazza d'Ara Coeli, to this elegant Michelangelo-designed piazza. At the top, the piazza is flanked by **Palazzo Nuovo** and **Palazzo dei Conservatori**, together home to the Capitoline Museums, and **Palazzo Senatorio**, seat of Rome City Council. In the centre, the **statue of Marcus Aurelius** is a copy of a 2nd-century bronze. (🚌 Piazza Venezia)

Capitoline Museums
MUSEUM

3 ◉ Map p30, A2

Dating to 1471, the Capitoline Museums (Musei Capitolini), the world's oldest national museums, house one of Italy's finest collections of classical sculpture. Crowd-pleasers include the iconic *Lupa capitolina* (Capitoline Wolf) and the *Galata morente*, a moving depiction of a dying Gaul warrior. There's also a fab picture gallery with masterpieces by big guns Titian, Tintoretto, Rubens, Van Dyck and Caravaggio. A second museum building is on the north side of the piazza. (www.museicapitolini.org; Piazza del Campidoglio 1; adult/reduced €12/10; ⏰9am-8pm Tue-Sun; 🚌 Piazza Venezia)

Chiesa di Santa Maria in Aracoeli
CHURCH

4 ◉ Map p30, A2

Atop the 14th-century Aracoeli staircase, this Romanesque gem is home to crisp 15th-century frescoes by Pinturicchio and the *santo bambino* (holy baby), a wooden baby Jesus believed to have healing powers. The original was pinched in 1994 but the copy apparently does the trick. (Piazza del Campidoglio 4; ⏰9am-12.30pm & 2.30-5.30pm; 🚌 Piazza Venezia)

Il Vittoriano
MONUMENT

5 ◉ Map p30, A1

Love it or loathe it, as most locals do, you can't ignore Il Vittoriano, the massive white marble monument to Italy's first king, Vittorio Emanuele II. Behind the Tomb of the Unknown Soldier, a **panoramic lift** (adult/reduced €7/3.50; ⏰9.30am-6.30pm Mon-Thu, to 7.30pm Fri-Sun) whisks you up to the rooftop and Rome's best 360-degree views. Last admission is 45 minutes before closing. (Piazza Venezia; admission free; ⏱9.30am-5.30pm summer, 9.30am-4.30pm winter; 🚇Piazza Venezia)

Mercati di Traiano Museo dei Fori Imperiali
MUSEUM

6 ◉ Map p30, B1

Housed in Trajan's 2nd-century shopping mall, this striking museum

showcases ancient artefacts found in the Imperial Forums. From the main hallway, a lift whisks you to the upper levels of the **Mercati di Traiano** (Trajan's Markets), a three-storey semicircular complex that once housed hundreds of traders selling everything from oil and vegetables to flowers, silks and spices. (www.mercatiditraiano.it; Via IV Novembre 94; adult/reduced €11/9; ⏱9am-7pm Tue-Sun; 🚇Via IV Novembre)

Imperial Forums
ANCIENT RUINS

7 ◉ Map p30, C2

The forums of Trajan, Augustus, Nerva and Caesar are known collectively as the Imperial Forums (Fori Imperiali). These were largely buried when Mussolini bulldozed Via dei Fori Imperiali through them in 1933 but excavations have since brought them back to light. The standout sight is the **Colonna di Traiano** (Trajan's Column), whose intricate reliefs depict Trajan's victories over the Dacians (from modern-day Romania). (Via dei Fori Imperiali; 🚇Via dei Fori Imperiali)

Museo Nazionale del Palazzo Venezia
MUSEUM

8 ◉ Map p30, A1

For hundreds of years the 15th-century Palazzo Venezia served as the embassy of the Venetian Republic. However, its most notorious resident was Mussolini, who famously made speeches from its balcony. Nowadays, it houses the Museo Nazionale

---

Understand
Romulus & Remus

According to legend, Romulus and Remus were the fruit of a steamy encounter between vestal virgin Rhea Silva and Mars, the god of war. Whilst still babies, they were set adrift on the Tiber to escape a death penalty imposed by their great-uncle, Amulius, who at the time was battling with their grandfather, Numitor, for control of Alba Longa. However, they were discovered near the Palatino by a clucky she-wolf, who suckled them until a shepherd found and raised them.

When Amulius later captured the unruly Remus, brother Romulus set him free, knocking off the king and paving the way for a city of their own. But the brotherly goodwill was short-lived: bickering over the new city walls drove Romulus to murder his brother and take full credit for the founding of Rome on 21 April 753 BC.

Medusa sculpture, Capitoline Museums (p31)

del Palazzo Venezia and its eclectic collection of Byzantine and early Renaissance paintings, camp ceramics, tapestries, arms and armour. (Via del Plebiscito 118; adult/reduced €4/2; ⏱8.30am-7.30pm Tue-Sun; 🚇Piazza Venezia)

Bocca della Verità   MONUMENT

9 ◉ Map p30, A4

The 'Mouth of Truth' is Rome's most famous lie detector. A mask-shaped marble disc that was once part of an ancient fountain, or possibly an ancient manhole cover, it's said to bite off the hand of fibbers. If you pass the test, pop into the adjoining 8th-century **Chiesa di Santa Maria in Cosmedin** for some stunning Cosmati interiors. (Piazza della Bocca della Verità 18; voluntary donation €0.50; ⏱9.30am-4.50pm winter, 9.30am-5.50pm summer; 🚇Via dei Cerchi)

Eating

Enoteca Provincia Romana   TRADITIONAL ITALIAN €€

10 🍴 Map p30, B1

Specialising in regional food and wine, this stylish wine bar-cum-restaurant offers a daily menu of pastas and mains, wine by the glass, finger foods and an evening aperitif. Service is friendly, and with an enviable location overlooking the Colonna di Traiano, it's a top choice. Lunchtime is busy but it quietens in the evening. (📞06 6994 0273; Foro Traiano 82-4; meals €35, aperitifs from €5; ⏱11am-11pm Mon-Sat; 🚇Via dei Fori Imperiali)

Understand

Ancient Rome – a History

Rome started life as an amalgamation of Etruscan, Latin and Sabine settlements on the Palatino, Esquilino and Quirinale hills. It was initially ruled by Sabine and Etruscan kings but the death of Tarquinius the Proud paved the way for the declaration of the Roman Republic in 509 BC.

The Republic
Under the Republic, Rome grew to become the Western world's undisputed superpower. Its armies conquered the Etruscans to the north and the Greeks and Carthaginians in the south. At home, it adopted a quasi-democratic system of government, based on a Senate and People's Assemblies – hence SPQR (Senatus Populusque Romanus, or the Senate and People of Rome). Roads were laid, including Via Appia Antica (Appian Way; p104), a thriving port was established at Ostia (p171) and a sophisticated network of aqueducts and underground sewers was built.

The Roman Empire
By the 1st century BC the Republic was in trouble and when Julius Caesar was assassinated in 44 BC it finally collapsed, giving rise to a vicious power struggle. Octavian emerged victorious and in 27 BC he took the hot seat as Rome's first emperor, Augustus. An enlightened ruler, he oversaw a period of peace and artistic development. But disaster was never far away and in AD 64 the city was devastated by a week-long fire. Nero blamed the Christians and executed many, including St Peter and St Paul. Yet the empire continued to flourish, and in about AD 100 it reached its zenith, stretching from Britannia to North Africa, and from Hispania to Syria.

   Decline set in during the 3rd century. Barbarian invasions led Aurelian to build his city walls and economic problems forced Diocletian to split the empire into eastern and western halves. Rivalries between the two empires culminated in the Battle of Milvian Bridge (312) and the accession of Constantine to the western throne. Constantine legalised Christianity before transferring to Byzantium (Istanbul) in 330, thus setting Rome on the route to ruin, which finally came in 476.

Alimentari Pannella Carmela
SANDWICH SHOP €

11 🍴 Map p30, A3

If you don't fancy a restaurant lunch, try a panino from this small food store, hidden in a quiet corner behind the Campidoglio. Choose your bread and filling from the array of rolls, hams and cheeses laid out on the counter or plump for ready-made salads or sliced pizza. (Via dei Fienili 61; panini €2; ⏲8.30am-2.30pm & 5-8pm Mon-Fri, 8.30am-2.30pm Sat; 🚌Via Petroselli)

San Teodoro
MODERN ITALIAN €€€

12 🍴 Map p30, A3

San Teodoro's formula for success is no secret: a romantic setting on a medieval piazza, local contemporary art, a quaffable wine list and sophisticated modern food. Sit in the cool, minimalist interior or outside on the covered terrace and enjoy creative seafood dishes and high-quality Roman classics. (🕿06 678 09 33; www.st-teodoro.it; Via dei Fienili 49-50; meals €80; ⏲Mon-Sat; 🚌Via Petroselli)

Drinking
Cavour 313
WINE BAR

13 🚇 Map p30, C2

A popped cork away from the Roman Forum, snug Cavour 313 charms everyone from ministers to fledgling Romeos. The 1200-label wine list spans low-cost locals to New World vintages, and are matched by yummy cheese platters, cold cuts and light meals. (www.cavour313.it; Via Cavour 313; ⏲12.30-2.45pm & 7.30pm-12.30am, closed Sun summer; Ⓜ Cavour)

Caffè Capitolino
CAFE

14 🚇 Map p30, A2

The Capitoline Museums' sleek cafe is a good place for a sightseeing time-out, although you don't need a ticket to drink here – it's accessible via an independent entrance on Piazzale Caffarelli. The light snacks (panini, salads and pizza) won't leave you breathless, but the charming rooftop setting will. (Piazzale Caffarelli 4; ⏲9am-7pm Tue-Sun; 🚌Piazza Venezia)

0,75
BAR

15 🚇 Map p30, B5

A welcoming bar on the Circo Massimo, good for a lingering drink, weekend brunch (€15, 11am to 3pm), *aperitivo* (aperitif), or a light lunch (pastas from €7, salads from €6.50). It's a friendly place with a laid-back vibe, an attractive exposed-brick look and cool tunes. Free wi-fi. (www.075roma.com; Via dei Cerchi 65; ⏲11am-2am; 🚌Via dei Cerchi; 🛜)

Explore

Centro Storico

Show-off piazzas, frescoed *palazzi* (mansions), cobbled alleyways, cafes and stylish bars: the tightly packed *centro storico* (historic centre) delivers the Rome you're most likely pining for. The Pantheon and Piazza Navona are the star turns, but you'll also find a host of monuments, museums and churches, many with works by Michelangelo, Caravaggio, Bernini et al.

The Sights in a Day

☀ Kick start your day with a coffee at **La Tazza d'Oro** (p50) before hitting the **Pantheon** (p38) early to avoid the crowds. Next, nip down to the **Chiesa di Santa Maria Sopra Minerva** (p45) to glimpse a minor Michelangelo before heading via **Piazza di Sant'Ignazio Loyola** (p45) to the **Galleria Doria Pamphilj** (p44) and its superb collection of Old Masters. That done, double back to **Armando al Pantheon** (p47) for an authentic Roman lunch.

☀ Recharged, push on to **Piazza Navona** (p44), Rome's showpiece baroque square. Nearby, the **Museo Nazionale Romano: Palazzo Altemps** (p44) houses some wonderful classical sculpture and the **Chiesa di San Luigi dei Francesi** (p44) boasts a trio of Caravaggios. To round off the day's sightseeing cross Corso Vittorio Emanuele II to check out **Campo de' Fiori** (p47) and **Palazzo Farnese** (p47).

☾ Spend the evening exploring the centre's animated backstreets. Dine on modern Italian fare at **Casa Coppelle** (p47), then join the beautiful people at **Salotto 42** (p51) or the neighbourhood gossips at **Caffè Sant'Eustachio** (p50).

For a local's day in the Centro Storico, see p40.

 Top Sights

Pantheon (p38)

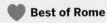 **Local Life**

A Day Out in the Centro Storico (p40)

💜 **Best of Rome**

Free

Piazza Navona (p44)

Chiesa di San Luigi dei Francesi (p44)

Chiesa di Santa Maria Sopra Minerva (p45)

Campo de' Fiori (p47)

Getting There

🚌 **Bus** The best way to access the area. From Termini, buses 40 and 64 stop at Largo di Torre Argentina and continue down Corso Vittorio Emanuele II.

Ⓜ **Metro** There are no metro stations in the neighbourhood but it's within walking distance of Barberini, Spagna and Flaminio stations to the east and north.

🚊 **Tram** Tram 8 connects Largo di Torre Argentina with Trastevere.

Top Sights
Pantheon

Along with the Colosseum, the Pantheon is one of Rome's iconic sights. A striking 2000-year-old temple, now church, it's the city's best-preserved ancient monument and one of the most influential buildings in the history of Western architecture. Built by Hadrian over Marcus Agrippa's earlier temple, it has stood since AD 120, and although the greying, pockmarked exterior is looking its age, it remains an exhilarating experience to enter and gaze upwards at the world's largest unreinforced concrete dome.

◉ Map p42, C3

Piazza della Rotonda

admission free

⊘ 8.30am-7.30pm Mon-Sat, 9am-6pm Sun

▣ Largo di Torre Argentina

Don't Miss

The Exterior
Showing signs of wear, the imposing portico is made up of 16 13m-high columns supporting a pediment. Little remains of the original decor but holes indicate where marble-veneer panels were once placed. The towering bronze doors are 16th-century restorations of the originals.

The Inscription
For centuries the inscription under the pediment led historians to believe that the current temple was Marcus Agrippa's original. The wording suggests so, reading: 'M.AGRIPPA.L.F.COS.TERTIUM. FECIT' or 'Marcus Agrippa, son of Lucius, consul for the third time, built this'. However, 19th-century excavations revealed traces of an earlier temple and scholars realised that Hadrian had simply kept Agrippa's original inscription.

The Interior
With light streaming in through the oculus (the hole in the centre of the dome), the marble-clad interior seems vast. Opposite the entrance is the main altar, while to the left are the tombs of artist Raphael, King Umberto I and Margherita of Savoy. On the opposite side of the rotunda is the tomb of King Vittorio Emanuele II.

The Dome
The Pantheon's dome, considered the Romans' most important architectural achievement, is the largest unreinforced concrete dome ever built. Its harmonious appearance is due to a precisely calibrated symmetry – the diameter is exactly equal to the building's interior height of 43.3m. Light (and rain) enters through the 8.7m-diameter oculus, which serves to absorb and redistribute the dome's huge tensile forces.

☑ **Top Tips**

▶ Avoid visiting during mass, which is celebrated at 5pm on Saturdays and 10.30am on public holidays.

▶ Visit around midday to see a beam of light stream in through the oculus.

▶ Look down as well as up – the sloping marble floor has 22 almost-invisible holes to drain away rain that gets in through the oculus.

▶ Return after dark for amazing views of the Pantheon set against the ink-blue night sky.

✕ **Take a Break**

The streets around the Pantheon are thick with eateries, cafes and bars. For an uplifting espresso, try La Tazza d'Oro (p50), one of the city's best coffee houses. For a quick gelato fix, make a beeline for Grom (p49).

Local Life
A Day Out in the Centro Storico

Rome's historic centre casts a powerful spell. But it's not just visitors who fall for its romantic piazzas, suggestive lanes, and street-side cafes. Away from the tourist spotlight, locals love to spend time here, shopping, unwinding over a drink, taking in an exhibition or simply hanging out with friends.

① An Exhibition at the Chiostro del Bramante

Tucked away in the backstreets near Piazza Navona, the Renaissance **Chiostro del Bramante** (Bramante Cloister; www.chiostrodelbramante.it; Vicolo dell'Arco della Pace 5; exhibitions adult/reduced €12/10; ⏰10am-8pm daily; 🚌Corso del Rinascimento) is a stunning setting for contemporary art exhibitions. Afterwards, pop

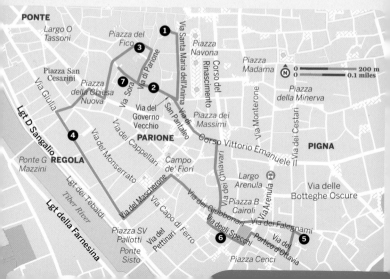

upstairs for a mid-morning coffee, light lunch or aperitif at the smart in-house cafe.

❷ Shopping around Via del Governo Vecchio

A charming street lined with arty boutiques, Via del Governo Vecchio strikes off **Piazza Pasquino**, home to a celebrated 'talking statue' (to which Romans used to stick notes lampooning the authorities). It can get touristy but locals love the vibe too and the area has some great shops, including trendy jeans store **SBU** (Via di San Pantaleo 68-69; 🕙10am-7.30pm Mon-Sat; 🚌Corso Vittorio Emanuele II).

❸ Lunch at Bar del Fico

Named after the fig tree that shades the chess-playing old boys outside, the laid-back **Bar del Fico** (Via della Pace 34-35; meals €15-20; 🕙8am-2am; 🚌Largo di Torre) is good any time of the day, from breakfast through to dinner. The big bowls of lunchtime pasta hit the spot nicely and the low-key boho decor – rough wooden floors, tin tables and grey, chipped walls – makes for a relaxed ambience.

❹ Stroll Via Giulia

Lined with Renaissance *palazzi* and potted orange trees, Via Giulia is a picture-perfect strip to stroll. At its southern end, the **Fontana del Mascherone** depicts a gobsmacked 17th-century hippie spewing water from his mouth. Close by, the ivy-dripping **Arco Farnese** was part of an ambitious, unfinished project to link two Farnese palaces.

❺ Spa Treatment in the Ghetto

Down in the Jewish Ghetto, **Acqua Madre Hamma** (www.acquamadre.it; Via di Sant'Ambrogio 17; hammam €50, massages from €60; 🕙2-9pm Tue, 11am-9pm Thu, Sat & Sun, women only 11am-9pm Wed & Fri; 🚌🚌Via Arenula) is a chic *hammam* (Turkish bath) where frazzled urbanites soak away their stresses and pamper themselves with seriously sublime massage and beauty treatments.

❻ Beer at Open Baladin

In recent years Rome has discovered beer and with more than 40 brews on tap and up to 100 bottled beers, **Open Baladin** (www.openbaladinroma.it; Via degli Specchi 5-6; 🕙noon-2am; 🚌🚌Via Arenula) is one of the scene's leading lights. A hip lounge bar, it specialises in Italian brews ranging from classic blondes and golden ales to lavender-infused concoctions.

❼ Pizza at Baffetto

For the full-on Roman pizza experience head back to Via del Governo Vecchio for dinner at **Pizzeria da Baffetto** (www.pizzeriadabaffetto.it; Via del Governo Vecchio 114; pizzas €6-9; 🕙6.30pm-1am; 🚌Corso Vittorio Emanuele II). Not everyone loves this historic pizzeria but if you're up for it, meals are raucous, chaotic and fast, and the thin-crust pizzas are spot on.

COLONNA

Piazza di San Silvestro

Palazzo Chigi

Via del Corso

Galleria Doria Pamphilj

Via della Gatta

Via del Corso

Piazza Colonna

Piazza di Pietra

Via di Pietra

Via di Sant'Ignazio

Piazza Grazioli

Palazzo di Montecitorio

Piazza di Montecitorio

Piazza del Parlamento

Via in Lucina

Via del Parlamento

Via del Leoncino

Via della Lupa

Via dei Prefetti

Via di Campo Marzio

Sant'Ignazio Loyola

Via del Gesù

Via del Piè di Marmo

PIGNA

Chiesa di Santa Maria Sopra Minerva

Piazza della Pigna

Piazza della Minerva

Via dei Cestari

Via del Seminario

Piazza della Rotonda

Pantheon

Via di Torre Argentina

Via delle Colonnelle

Via degli Orfani

Via della Maddalena

Piazza della Maddalena

Via della Scrofa

Via della Lupa

Piazza delle Coppelle

Via delle Coppelle

Largo G Toniolo

Via Giustiniani

Salita dei Crescenzi

Via Monterone

Via della Dogana Vecchia

Via dei Crescenzi

Via del Teatro Valle

Piazza Sant'Andrea della Valle

Via Melone

Piazza Nicosia

Via della Scrofa

Via di Monte Brianzo

Via dell'Orso

Via dei Portoghesi

Palazzo Altemps

Museo Nazionale Romano: Palazzo Altemps

Piazza Sant'Apollinare

Piazza di Sant'Agostino

Via delle Cinque Lune

Chiesa di Sant'Agostino

Chiesa di San Luigi dei Francesi

Corso del Rinascimento

Piazza dei Massimi

Lgt Marzio

COLONNA

Lgt Castello

Ponte Umberto I

Lgt Tor di Nona

Via Zanardelli

Via dei Soldati

Via Tor Sanguigna

Piazza Navona

Piazza Santa Maria dell'Anima

Via Santa Maria dell'Anima

Via dei Canestrari

Piazza Lacellotti

Via dei Coronari

Via di Parione

PARIONE

Via del Governo Vecchio

Via Sora

Corso Vittorio Emanuele II

Piazza di San Marco

Piazza del Plebiscito

Via degli Astalli

Via di San Marco

Piazza d'Ara Coeli

Via del Teatro di Marcello

Via Mananara

Piazza del Chiesa del Gesù

Via d'Aracoeli

Via del Gesù

◎ 5

Via Celsa

Piazza Capizucchi

Via delle Botteghe Oscure

Museo Nazionale Romano: Cripta Balbi

◎ 8

Via M Caetani

Via de Delfini

Piazza Montanara

Via Montanara

SANT'ANGELO

Via del Foro Piscario

Teatro di Marcello

✕ 20

Largo di Torre Argentina

Via di Torre Argentina

Via Florida

Via delle Botteghe Oscure

Largo Arenula

Via Arenula

Via dei Falegnami

Piazza Costaguti

Via del Portico d'Ottavia

Via Santa Maria dei Calderari

Via Catalana

◎ 27

Ponte Fabricio

Isola Tiberina

Ponte Cesto

Via del Sudario

Via dei Barbieri

Via di Sant'Anna

Via dei Giubbonari

Piazza B Cairoli

Via San Bartolomeo dei Vaccinari

Lgt de Cenci

Lgt degli Anguillara

◎ 30

Via dei Chiavari

Via dei Librari

Largo dei Librari

✕ 34

◎ 14

Via degli Specchi

Via delle Zoccolette

Via di SantaSeggiola

Lgt D Sangalio

Lgt dei Vallati

Ponte Garibaldi

Piazza del Teatro di Pompeo

Piazza del Biscione

Campo de' Fiori

Via dei Baullari

◎ 10

Via del Pellegrino

Vic delle Grotte

Piazza del Trinità Pelegrini

◎ 33

Via Capo di Ferro

Palazzo Spada

Via dei Pettinari

Via dei Conservatorio

Ponte Sisto

Lgt Raphaello Sanzio

Tiber River

Via del Politeama

✕ 15

Piazza Farnese

◎ 9

Palazzo Farnese

Via dei Farnesi

Via Giulia

Lgt dei Tebaldi

200 m

0.1 miles

N

5

6

7

8

E

D

C

B

A

Sights

Piazza Navona
PIAZZA

 Map p42, B3

Sun-roasted *palazzi*, extravagant fountains, street artists and spritz-sipping poseurs: Rome's most iconic piazza sits atop the 1st-century-AD Stadio di Domiziano. Its centrepiece is Bernini's **Fontana dei Quattro Fiumi** (Fountain of the Four Rivers), which looks towards the Borromini-designed **Chiesa di Sant'Agnese in Agone** (www.santagneseinagone.org; ⊙9.30am-12.30pm & 4-7pm Tue-Sun), a baroque classic that hosts regular chamber-music concerts. (🚇Corso del Rinascimento)

Galleria Doria Pamphilj
GALLERY

2 Map p42, E4

One of Rome's richest private art collections is housed in the mid-15th-century Palazzo Doria Pamphilj, which is still home to Rome's aristocratic Pamphilj family. With works by Raphael, Tintoretto, Brueghel, Titian, Caravaggio, Bernini and Velázquez, masterpieces abound, but the collection's undisputed star is the Velázquez portrait of Pope Innocent X. (www.dopart.it; Via del Corso 305; adult/reduced €11/7.50; ⊙9am-7pm; 🚇Piazza Venezia)

Museo Nazionale Romano: Palazzo Altemps
MUSEUM

3 Map p42, B2

Heavenly bodies fill the frescoed rooms of this exquisite Renaissance palace, home to Cardinal Ludovico Ludovisi's celebrated sculpture collection. Prize exhibits include the mesmerising 6th-century *Galata suicida* (Gaul's Suicide) and the 5th-century-BC *Trono Ludovisi* (Ludovisi Throne). The museum also houses the Museo Nazionale Romano's Egyptian collection. (Piazza Sant'Apollinare 46; adult/reduced incl Crypta Balbi, Palazzo Massimo & Terme di Diocleziano €7/3.50, plus possible €3 exhibition supplement; ⊙9am-7.45pm Tue-Sun; 🚇Corso del Rinascimento)

Chiesa di San Luigi dei Francesi
CHURCH

4 Map p42, C3

Caravaggio connoisseurs are spoilt rotten at Rome's French national church, with three of the master's canvases hanging in the Cappella Contarelli. Known as the St Matthew cycle (1600–02), they showcase Caravaggio's astounding mastery of chiaroscuro (the bold contrast of light and dark). A lesser-known highlight is Domenichino's 17th-century frescoes in the second chapel on the right. (Piazza di San Luigi dei Francesi; ⊙10am-12.30pm & 3-7pm Fri-Wed, 10am-12.30pm Thu; 🚇Corso del Rinascimento)

Chiesa del Gesù
CHURCH

5 Map p42, D5

Rome's first Jesuit church is a bombastic 16th-century Counter-Reformation extravaganza, starring Giovanni Battista Gaulli's swirling vault fresco

Chiesa di San Luigi dei Francesi

Triumph of the Name of Jesus. Equally opulent is Andrea del Pozzo's tomb for Jesuit founder Ignatius Loyola, who lived in the church from 1544 until his death in 1556 – his private **rooms** (⏱4-6pm Mon-Sat, 10am-noon Sun) are right of the main church. (Piazza del Gesù; ⏱7am-12.30pm & 4-7.45pm; 🚊🚌Largo di Torre Argentina)

Chiesa di Santa Maria Sopra Minerva
CHURCH

 6 👁 Map p42, D4

Bernini's much-loved **Elefantino** sculpture trumpets the presence of Rome's only Gothic church. Dating to the 13th century, it boasts electric-blue vaulting and Renaissance gems such as Filippino Lippi frescoes,

Fra Angelico's tomb and Michelangelo's *Cristo risorto* (Christ Bearing the Cross). The body of St Catherine of Siena, minus her head (which is in Siena), is also here, under the high altar. (Piazza della Minerva; ⏱8am-7pm Mon-Fri, 8am-1pm & 3.30-7pm Sat & Sun; 🚊🚌Largo di Torre Argentina)

Piazza di Sant'Ignazio Loyola
PIAZZA

7 👁 Map p42, E3

Laid out in 1727 to resemble a theatrical set, complete with exits into 'the wings', this exquisite rococo piazza is home to the 17th-century **Chiesa di Sant'Ignazio di Loyola** (⏱7.30am-7pm Mon-Sat, 9am-7pm Sun), an important Jesuit church celebrated for Andrea

Understand
Art & Architecture in Rome

In Rome you're constantly surrounded by great art and architecture. Walk around the centre and even without trying you'll stumble across masterpieces by Renaissance heroes and extravagant baroque beauties.

The Renaissance
The Renaissance swept into Rome in the late 15th century, unleashing a massive overhaul of the medieval city. Leading the way was the architect Bramante, whose work on St Peter's Basilica (p138) was developed by Michelangelo, author of the basilica's dome and the spectacular frescoes in the Sistine Chapel (p143). Artists, inspired by humanist philosophies, focused much energy on the depiction of the human form, resulting in two of the era's headline works: Michelangelo's *Pietà* in St Peter's Basilica (p139) and Raphael's *La scuola di Atene* in the Vatican Museums (p145).

Baroque Flair
Emerging out of the Counter-Reformation, baroque art and architecture was dynamic, emotional and religiously inspired. Martyrdoms, ecstasies and miracles were depicted, and churches became increasingly ornamental. The key players were Gian Lorenzo Bernini, Francesco Borromini, and Caravaggio, whose lifelike portrayal of hitherto sacrosanct subjects caused uproar – such as his St Matthew cycle in the Chiesa di San Luigi dei Francesi (p44). Bernini and Borromini were more mainstream in their approach – Bernini's sculptures in the Museo e Galleria Borghese (p156) and Borromini's Chiesa di San Carlo alle Quattro Fontane (p72) are definitive examples of their style.

Modern Times
The 20th century gave rise to two important movements: rationalism, a linear form of architecture that found full expression in EUR (p177); and futurism, a modernist abstract style that you can explore at the Galleria Nazionale d'Arte Moderna (p160). More recently, a number of high-profile building projects have been completed in the city: Renzo Piano's Auditorium Parco della Musica (p163), the Zaha Hadid–designed Museo Nazionale delle Arti del XXI Secolo (MAXXI; p183) and Odile Decq's Museo d'Arte Contemporanea di Roma (MACRO; p161).

Pozzo's trompe l'œil ceiling fresco. For the best views, look up from the small yellow spot on the nave floor. (🚇Via del Corso)

Museo Nazionale Romano: Crypta Balbi
MUSEUM

8 ◎ Map p42, D6

Built around medieval and Renaissance ruins, themselves plonked on top of the 1st-century-BC Theatre of Balbus, this oft-overlooked museum vividly illustrates Rome's multilayered history. Duck into the underground excavations, and view well-labelled exhibitions, complete with 6th-century bling and Byzantine toys. (Via delle Botteghe Oscure 31; adult/reduced incl Palazzo Altemps, Palazzo Massimo & Terme di Diocleziano €7/3.50, plus possible €3 exhibition supplement; ⏱9am-7.45pm Tue-Sun; 🚇🚌Largo di Torre Argentina)

Palazzo Farnese
HISTORICAL BUILDING

9 ◎ Map p42, A6

Home to the French embassy, this 16th-century palace is the work of Antonio da Sangallo, Michelangelo and Giacomo della Porta. Inside, Annibale Carracci's astounding frescoes are said to rival those of the Sistine Chapel. Visits are by guided tour only, for which you'll need to book at least a week in advance. Photo ID is required for entry; children under 10 are not admitted. (www.inventerrome.com; Piazza Farnese; admission €5; ⏱45min tours Mon, Wed & Fri; 🚇Corso Vittorio Emanuele II)

Campo de' Fiori
PIAZZA

10 ◎ Map p42, B5

By day, Rome's only churchless square is a colourful spectacle of heaving market stalls. By night, 'Il Campo' becomes an open-air party, its vaguely trashy pubs and bars overflowing with revellers. No doubt many a sleepless local wishes them the fate of heretical monk Giordano Bruno, burnt here in 1600 and honoured by Ettore Ferrari's sinister statue. (🚇Corso Vittorio Emanuele II)

Eating

Casa Coppelle
MEDITERRANEAN €€

11 🍴 Map p42, C2

Exposed-brick walls, books, flowers and subdued lighting set the stage for wonderful French-inspired food at this intimate, romantic restaurant. There's a full range of starters and pastas but the real tour de force is the steak, which is cooked superbly and served with thinly sliced potato crisps. Book ahead. (📞06 6889 1707; www.casacoppelle.it; Piazza delle Coppelle 49; meals €35; 🚇🚌Largo di Torre Argentina)

Armando al Pantheon
TRATTORIA €€

12 🍴 Map p42, C3

An institution in these parts, Armando is a rare find – a genuine family-run trattoria in the touristy Pantheon area. It's been on the go for more than

50 years and has served its fair share of celebs – philosopher Jean-Paul Sartre and Brazilian footballer Pelé have both eaten here – but the focus remains on traditional, earthy Roman food. (☎06 6880 3034; www.armandoal pantheon.it; Salita dei Crescenzi 31; meals €35-40; ☺lunch & dinner Mon-Fri, lunch Sat; 🚌🚊Largo di Torre Argentina)

La Rosetta SEAFOOD €€€

13 Map p42, C3

Supreme seafood, superlative service and a refreshing lack of pretension keep this legendary fish restaurant in the 'bookings only' league. Secure a spot and swoon over classics such as seafood linguine and more elaborate ensembles such as hot scampi salad with leeks, lime and chickpeas. It's closed for three weeks in August. (☎06 686 10 02; www.larosetta.com; Via della Rosetta 8-9; meals €90, menu €120; ☺lunch & dinner daily; 🚌🚊Largo di Torre Argentina)

Forno Roscioli BAKERY, PIZZA AL TAGLIO €

14 Map p42, B6

This is one of Rome's top bakeries, much loved by lunching locals who crowd here for luscious *pizza al taglio* (pizza by the slice). But there's more than just pizza, with fresh-from-the-oven treats such as *crostate* (fruit tarts), *tortine di ricotta e cioccolato* (ricotta-and-chocolate mini cakes) and *taralli* (a pretzel-like snack from the southern Puglia region). (Via dei Chiavari 34; pizza slices from €2; ☺7.30am-8pm Mon-Fri, 7.30am-2.30pm Sat; 🚌🚊Via Arenula)

Forno di Campo de' Fiori BAKERY, PIZZA AL TAGLIO €

15 Map p42, A5

This ever-buzzing bakery makes obscenely good *pizza al taglio*, as well as panini and savoury snacks. There are two branches on either side of Via dei Cappellari on Campo de' Fiori. Grab a slice or three of *pizza bianca* – pizza with olive oil, rosemary and salt – pair it with an *occhio di bue* (apricot-jam

---

⊙ **Local Life**
Jewish Ghetto

Centred on lively Via del Portico d'Ottavia, the **Jewish Ghetto** (Map p42; D7; 🚌🚊Via Arenula) is an atmospheric area studded with artisans studios, vintage-clothes shops, kosher bakeries and popular trattorias. Highlights include the **Area Archeologica del Teatro di Marcello e del Portico D'Ottavia** (Via del Teatro di Marcello 44; admission free; ☺9am-7pm summer, to 6pm winter; 🚌Via del Teatro di Marcello) and its Colosseum-clone, Teatro di Marcello, and the **Museo Ebraico di Roma** (www.museoebraico.roma.it; Lungotevere de Cenci; adult/reduced €10/7.50; ☺10am-6.15pm Sun-Thu, 10am-3.15pm Fri, shorter hr winter; 🚌Lungotevere de Cenci), which chronicles the city's Jewish history. Nearby, the **Isola Tiberina** is the world's smallest inhabited island.

tartlet) and munch to your heart's content on the piazza outside. (☎06 6880 6662; Campo de' Fiori 22; pizza slices €3; ⏱7.30am-2.30pm & 4.45-8pm Mon-Sat; 🚍Corso Vittorio Emanuele II)

Grom   GELATERIA €

16 Map p42, C2

With branches all over Italy as well as Paris, New York and Tokyo, this gourmet gelato chain is renowned for its high-quality, additive-free ice cream. Flavours run the gamut from classics made from seasonal fruit and South American chocolate, to exotica flavoured with Chinese tea, Calabrian liquorice, Himalayan pink salt and other prized ingredients. (www.grom.it; Via della Maddalena 30; cones from €2.50; ⏱11am-1am Mon-Thu, 11am-1.30am Fri & Sat, 10am-1am Sun summer, shorter hr winter; 🚍Largo di Torre Argentina)

Cul de Sac   TRATTORIA €€

17 Map p42, B4

A popular little *enoteca* (wine bar), just off Piazza Navona, with an always-busy terrace and narrow, bottle-lined interior. Choose from the encyclopedic wine list and ample menu of Gallic-inspired soups, cold cuts, pâtés, cheeses and main courses. Book ahead in the evening. (☎06 6880 1094; www.enotecaculdesac.com; Piazza Pasquino 73; meals €30; ⏱noon-4pm & 6pm-12.30am; 🚍Corso Vittorio Emanuele II)

Casa Bleve   GASTRONOMIC €€€

18 Map p42, C4

Ideal for a romantic or Epicurean assignation, this gorgeous gastro delight dazzles with its column-lined courtyard and stained-glass roof. Its wine list, one of the best in town, accompanies hard-to-find cheeses and cold cuts, while in the evening there's a full à la carte menu of creative Italian dishes. It's closed for three weeks in August. (☎06 686 59 70; Via del Teatro Valle 48-49; meals €65; ⏱Tue-Sat; 🚍🚍Largo di Torre Argentina)

Giolitti   GELATERIA, PASTRIES & CAKES €

19 Map p42, D2

Rome's most famous gelateria keeps the hordes happy with succulent, natural-tasting sorbets and richer must-licks such as marrons glacés and hazelnut. Gregory Peck and Audrey Hepburn swung by in *Roman Holiday* and, more recently, Barack Obama's daughters popped in during a G8 summit. (Via degli Uffici del Vicario 40; ⏱7am-1am; 🚍Via del Corso)

Giggetto al Portico d'Ottavia   TRADITIONAL ITALIAN €€

20 Map p42, D7

For a crash course in Roman-Jewish flavours, dive into this ghetto landmark, famed for its deep-fried *carciofi* (artichokes) and *fiori di zucca*

CHRISTOPHER GROENHOUT/LONELY PLANET IMAGES ©

Market at Campo de' Fiori (p47)

(courgette flowers fried and flavoured with anchovies). If you can, bag an outside table next to the 1st-century Portico d'Ottavia. (☎06 686 11 05; Via del Portico d'Ottavia 21-22; meals €40; ⏰Tue-Sun; ☒☒Piazza Cairoli)

Drinking

Caffè Sant'Eustachio   CAFE

21 ☕ Map p42, C3

The coffee served at this small, unassuming cafe enjoys cult status. Created by beating the first drops of espresso and several teaspoons of sugar into a frothy paste, then adding the rest of the coffee on top, it's sweet, smooth and dangerously addictive.

Specify if you want it *amaro* (bitter) or *poco zucchero* (with a little sugar). (Piazza Sant'Eustachio 82; ⏰8.30am-1am Sun-Thu, to 1.30am Fri, to 2am Sat; ☒Corso del Rinascimento)

La Tazza d'Oro   CAFE

22 ☕ Map p42, D3

'The Golden Cup' is a title contender for Rome's best coffee house. Its espresso hits the mark perfectly and there's a range of delicious coffee concoctions, such as *granita di caffè*, a crushed-ice coffee with a big dollop of cream, and *parfait di caffè*, a €3 coffee mousse. (Via degli Orfani 84-86; ⏰7am-8pm Mon-Sat, 10.30am-7.30pm Sun; ☒Via del Corso)

Etablì

WINE BAR

23 Map p42, A3

A chic lounge-bar-restaurant, laid-back Etablì pairs French antiques with chandeliers, a crackling fireplace and a low-key urbane crowd. Slip into an armchair with a glass of red, nibble on fabulous *aperitivi* (aperitifs), or tuck into Roman/Mediterranean cuisine. Restaurant meals average €35 to €40. (www.etabli.it; Vicolo delle Vacche 9a; ⏱6.30pm-1am Mon-Wed, to 2am Thu-Sat; 🚌Corso del Rinascimento)

Salotto 42

BAR

24 Map p42, D2

On a picturesque piazza facing the columns of a 2nd-century Roman temple, the Tempio di Adriano, this slinky lounge bar has modernity on the mind – think suede lounges, vintage armchairs and designer tomes lining the walls. Come for the daily lunch buffet or to hang out with the beautiful people over an aperitif. Also brunch on Sunday. (www.salotto42.it; Piazza di Pietra 42; ⏱10am-2am Tue-Sat, to midnight Sun & Mon; 🚌Via del Corso)

Barnum Cafe

CAFE

25 Map p42, A4

If your idea of a cafe involves eclectic furniture, contemporary art and the odd design magazine to flick through, Barnum has your name all over its cool white brickwork. Sip on freshly squeezed orange juice as you sink into a tatty old armchair and ponder your next move. Light lunches are served and aperitif starts at 7pm. (www.barnumcafe.com; Via del Pellegrino 87; ⏱9.30am-9pm Mon, to 2am Tue-Sat; 🚌Corso Vittorio Emanuele II)

Il Goccetto

WINE BAR

26 Map p42, A4

Had anyone decided to make an Italian version of *Cheers,* it would have been recorded at this wood-panelled number, where a colourful cast of regulars finish each other's sentences, banter with the owners and work their way through the 800-strong wine list. Eavesdrop over plates of prized north Italian cheese and salami. (Via dei Banchi Vecchi 14; ⏱6.30pm-midnight Mon, 11.30am-2pm & 6.30pm-midnight Tue-Sat; 🚌Corso Vittorio Emanuele II)

Bartaruga

BAR

27 Map p42, D6

VIPs, theatre darlings and bohemians adore this snug, ghetto classic, with its mock-baroque ensemble of antique divans, velvet fabrics and Liberty wall lamps. Outside, a few humble tables face onto the ghetto's much-loved turtle fountain, the *Fontana delle tartarughe.* No credit cards. (www .bartaruga.com; Piazza Mattei 9; ⏱6pm-1am Tue-Thu, to 2am Fri & Sat, to midnight Sun; 🚌🚋Via Arenula)

Fluid
BAR

28 Map p42, A3

Glowing ice-cube stools, glass floor panels and ink-infused tabletops set a sleek scene at this popular evening hangout, where a tasty, abundant *aperitivo* spread (6pm to 8pm) meets well-mixed drinks, slinky DJ tunes and a chatty, chilled, eye-candy crowd. (Via del Governo Vecchio 46; ⏰6pm-2am; Corso del Rinascimento)

Caffe della Pace
CAFE, BAR

29 Map p42, A3

Live the *dolce vita* cliché at this perennially fashionable art nouveau cafe, complete with ivy-clad facade, alfresco tables for poseurs to people-watch over their Camparis, and a cosy interior. (Via della Pace 5; ⏰4pm-3am Mon, 9am-3am Tue-Sun; Corso Vittorio Emanuele II)

Entertainment

Teatro Argentina
THEATRE

30 Map p42, C5

Opened in 1792, Rome's top theatre is a lavish affair, decked out with red-curtained boxes and a garlanded frescoed ceiling. Rossini's *Barber of Seville* debuted here and its theatre program spans Shakespeare to Ray Bradbury (mostly in Italian). It occasionally hosts major dance productions, best booked early. (☎06 684 00 03; www.teatrodiroma.net; Largo di Torre Argentina 52; tickets €12-27; Largo di Torre Argentina)

Shopping

Confetteria Moriondo & Gariglio
CONFECTIONERY

31 Map p42, D4

Roman poet Trilussa was so smitten with this historic candy shop – established by the Torinese confectioners to the royal house of Savoy – that he dedicated several sonnets in its honour. Many of the handmade chocolates and bonbons, laid out in ceremonial splendour in old-fashioned glass cabinets, are still made to 19th-century recipes. (Via del Piè di Marmo 21-22; ⏰9am-7.30pm Mon-Sat; Via del Corso)

Arsenale
FASHION

32 Map p42, A4

A watchword with female fashionistas, Arsenale is a cool, contemporary boutique showcasing clothes by the ever-popular Roman designer Patrizia Pieroni. Her artistic designs, cut from rich, luscious fabrics, hang in the virgin-white interior alongside heavy rustic fittings. (www.patriziapieroni.it; Via del Pellegrino 172; ⏰10am-7.30pm Tue-Sat, 3.30-7.30pm Mon; Corso Vittorio Emanuele II)

Borini
SHOES

33 Map p42, B6

Don't be fooled by the piles of boxes and the workaday look – those in the know pile into this seemingly down-at-heel shop for the latest foot candy. Whatever shoes are 'in' this season,

Borini will have them, at reasonable prices and in every hue. (Via dei Pettinari 86-87; 🕐9am-1pm Tue-Sat & 3.30-7.30pm Mon-Sat; 🚌🚊Via Arenula)

Ibiz – Artigianato in Cuoio   ACCESSORIES

34 🔒 Map p42, B6

In their diminutive workshop, Elisa Nepi and her father craft exquisite, well-priced leather goods in simple but classy designs and myriad colours. With €40 you should be able to pick up a wallet, purse or pair of sandals; bags start at around €100. (Via dei Chiavari 39; 🕐9.30am-7.30pm Mon-Sat; 🚌Corso Vittorio Emanuele II)

Nardecchia   ANTIQUES

35 🔒 Map p42, B3

You'll be inviting people to see your etchings after a visit to this historic Piazza Navona shop. Famed for its antique prints, Nardecchia sells everything from exclusive 18th-century etchings by Giovanni Battista Piranesi to more affordable 19th-century panoramas. (Piazza Navona 25; 🕐10am-1pm Tue-Sat & 4.30-7.30pm Mon-Sat; 🚌Corso del Rinascimento)

Tempi Moderni   JEWELLERY

36 🔒 Map p42, A4

Bart Simpson ties and Ferragamo fashions sit side by side at Tempi Moderni, a kooky curiosity shop packed with art nouveau and art deco trinkets, costume jewellery, poptastic bangles and chichi options from the likes of Chanel, Balenciaga and Dior. (Via del Governo Vecchio 108; 🕐9am-1.30pm & 3-8pm Mon-Sat; 🚌Corso Vittorio Emanuele II)

Explore

Tridente

Tridente is unapologetically glam, full of big-name boutiques, debonair bars and top-end restaurants. Fashion pilgrims head to Via dei Condotti while tourists grab five on the Spanish Steps and people-watch on Piazza del Popolo, one of Rome's great piazzas. Art lovers can get their fill at the Renaissance Chiesa di Santa Maria del Popolo and modernist Museo dell'Ara Pacis.

The Sights in a Day

☀ Wake up with breakfast at **Caffè Greco** (p63), the one-time refuge of Romantic poets and Casanova, the legendary Lothario. From there, head up to **Piazza di Spagna** and the **Spanish Steps** (p56). Climb the staircase to the **Chiesa della Trinità dei Monti** (p57) and you're rewarded with wonderful rooftop views. Take your photos and double back to search out **Via Margutta** (p59), the charming traffic-free street that Federico Fellini once called home. Follow on to **Piazza del Popolo** (p59) and the art-rich **Chiesa di Santa Maria del Popolo** (p59).

☀ After lunch at bustling **'Gusto** (p61), head to the nearby **Museo dell'Ara Pacis** (pictured left; p59) to admire ancient Roman stonework in a cool, contemporary setting. Afterwards, reward yourself with some retail therapy, browsing the chain stores and boutiques on Via del Corso, Via dei Condotti and Via del Babuino (p64).

☾ Start the evening with an *aperitivo* (aperitif) at **La Scena** (p62) before a brasserie-styled dinner at **Babette** (p60). Round the day off by celeb-watching over cocktails at the **Stravinskij Bar at Hotel de Russie** (p63).

👁 Top Sights

Spanish Steps & Piazza di Spagna (p56)

♥ Best of Rome

Free
Spanish Steps (p56)

Piazza del Popolo (p59)

Chiesa di Santa Maria del Popolo (p59)

Shopping
Eleonora (p64)

Bomba (p64)

Fausto Santini (p64)

Gente (p64)

Fabriano (p64)

Furla (p65)

Getting There

Ⓜ **Metro** The easiest way to get to the district. Get off at Spagna (line A) for Piazza di Spagna, the Spanish Steps and Via dei Condotti, or at Flaminio for Piazza del Popolo.

🚌 **Bus** Bus 117 runs down part of Via del Corso as it connects Piazza del Popolo with Piazza di San Giovanni in Laterano.

Top Sights
Spanish Steps & Piazza di Spagna

Rising above Piazza di Spagna, the Spanish Steps (Scalinata di Trinità dei Monti) are a favourite hang-out for footsore tourists, migrant hawkers and preening local teens. Posing has a long and noble history here and when Dickens visited in the 19th century he reported that artists' models would hang around in the hope of being hired for a painting. The area has long been a magnet to foreigners and in the late 1700s it was known as *er ghetto de l'inglesi* (the English ghetto).

Map p58, D4

Piazzá di Spagna

admission free

M Spagna

Don't Miss

The Steps

A monumental 135-step staircase, the Spanish Steps are an early example of pan-European cooperation. Built in 1725 to a design by an Italian, Francesco de Sanctis, they were financed by French money and named after the nearby Spanish Embassy to the Holy See. At the top stands the Chiesa della Trinità dei Monti.

Chiesa della Trinità dei Monti

This landmark **church** (☉6am-8pm Tue-Sun) was commissioned by King Louis XII of France and consecrated in 1585. Apart from the great rooftop views from outside, it boasts some important mannerist frescoes by Daniele da Volterra.

Piazza di Spagna

Flanking the steps is the *palazzo* (mansion) where Romantic poet John Keats lived the last year of his life (see p59). Opposite, **Via dei Condotti** is Rome's most exclusive shopping strip, while to the southeast, adjacent **Piazza Mignanelli** is dominated by the **Colonna dell'Immacolata**, built in 1857 to celebrate Pope Pius IX's declaration of the Immaculate Conception.

Barcaccia

At the foot of the steps, the fountain of a sinking boat, the *Barcaccia* (1627), is believed to be by Pietro Bernini, father of the more famous Gian Lorenzo. It's fed from a low-pressure aqueduct, hence the low-key nature of the central fountain. Bees and suns decorate the structure, symbols of the Barberini family, who commissioned it.

☑ Top Tips

▶ To catch the steps in full bloom, visit in mid-April, when they're decorated with up to 600 vases of brightly coloured azaleas.

▶ Steer clear of the piazza on Saturday afternoons, when it's full of adolescents on heat.

▶ If you don't fancy climbing the steps, take the lift from the entrance/exit of Spagna metro station.

▶ Officially, you're not allowed to eat on the steps.

✕ Take a Break

Duck out of the piazza and head to nearby Gina (p62) to leave the crowds behind and indulge in a stylish snack or light lunch. Alternatively, recharge your batteries with a glass of wine at the Antica Enoteca (p61).

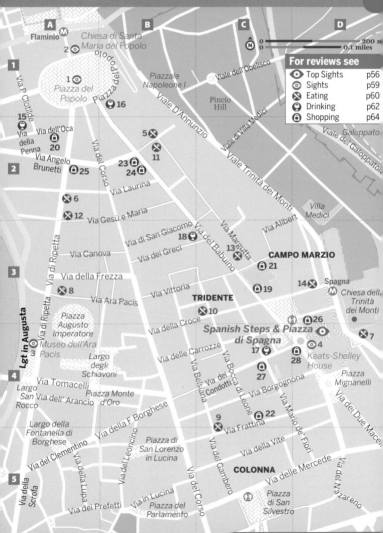

Flaminio M

A Chiesa di Santa
Maria del Popolo **B**

2 Chiesa di Santa

1 Piazza del
Popolo

16

Piazzale
Napoleone I

Viale dell'Obelisco

Pincio
Hill

C **D**

0   200 m
0   0.1 miles

Viale di Villa Medici

Viale Galoppato
Viale del Galoppatoio

For reviews see
◎ Top Sights   p56
◉ Sights   p59
✕ Eating   p60
◖ Drinking   p62
🔒 Shopping   p64

15
Via
della
Penna 20

Via dell'Oca

Via Angelo
Brunetti   25

23
24

5
11

Viale Trinità dei Monti

Villa
Medici

6
12

Via Laurina

Via Gesù e Maria

Via di San Giacomo

Via dei Greci

Via Canova

Via della Frezza

18

13

Via del Babuino

Via Margutta

Via Alibert

CAMPO MARZIO
21

8

Via Ara Pacis

Via Vittoria

19

14

Spagna
M Chiesa dell
Trinità
dei Monti

TRIDENTE
10

Piazza
Augusto
Imperatore

3 Museo dell'Ara
Pacis

Largo
degli
Schiavoni

Via della Croce

**Spanish Steps & Piazza
di Spagna**
17

26

7

4

Keats-Shelley
House

Via delle Carrozze

Via Tomacelli

Largo
San Via dell' Arancio
Rocco

Piazza Monte
d'Oro

Largo della
Fontanella di
Borghese

Via del Clementino

Via Belsiana

Via delle Carrozze

28

27

Via di
Bocca di Leone

Via dei
Condotti

Via Borgognona

Piazza
Mignanelli

Via dei Due Mace

9
Via Frattina

22

Via Mario de' Fiori

Piazza di
San Lorenzo
in Lucina

Via della Vite

COLONNA

Via del Gambero

Via delle Mercede

Via del Nazareno

Via della
Scrofa

Via dei Prefetti

Via in Lucina

Piazza del
Parlamento

Via del Corso

Piazza
di San
Silvestro

Sights

Piazza del Popolo   PIAZZA

1 ⊙ Map p58, A1

For centuries, this dashing piazza – styled in neoclassical splendour in the 19th century – was the site of public executions and the city's main northern gateway. Guarding its southern entrance are Carlo Rainaldi's not-quite-identical baroque churches, whilst opposite is the Bernini-designed **Porta del Popolo**. In the centre, the 36m-high Egyptian **obelisk** was moved here in the mid-16th century. (M Flaminio)

Chiesa di Santa Maria del Popolo   CHURCH

2 ⊙ Map p58, A1

Built to exorcise the ghost of Nero, which was said to haunt the area, this is one of Rome's richest Renaissance churches, with vault frescoes by Pinturicchio, two Caravaggios, and Rome's first stained-glass windows (1509) in the Bramante-designed apse. Raphael and Bernini are also represented – the former designed the Chigi chapel which the latter finished in the mid-17th century. (Piazza del Popolo; ⊙ 7.30am-noon & 4-7pm; M Flaminio)

Museo dell'Ara Pacis   MUSEUM

3 ⊙ Map p58, A4

Set inside Richard Meier's controversial modernist pavilion, the 1st-century-BC Ara Pacis Augustae (Altar of Peace) is a vast marble altar laden with exquisitely carved reliefs in honour of peacemaker emperor Augustus. Across the street, the once-glorious 28 BC **Mausoleo di Augusto** is the burial site of the emperor and his favourite nephew, Marcellus. (www.arapacis.it; Lungotevere in Augusta; adult/reduced €8.50/6.50; ⊙ 9am-7pm Tue-Sun; 🚌 Lungotevere in Augusta)

Keats-Shelley House   MUSEUM

4 ⊙ Map p58, D4

The Keats-Shelley House is where 25-year-old John Keats coughed his last in February 1821. The following year, his partner-in-verse Percy Bysshe Shelley drowned off the Tuscan coast. Snoop through atmospheric, stuck-in-time rooms crammed with memorabilia from the poets' short lives, including letters from Mary Shelley and Keats' death mask. (www.keats-shelley-house.org; Piazza di Spagna 26; adult/reduced €4.50/3.50; ⊙ 10am-1pm & 2-6pm Mon-Fri, 11am-2pm & 3-6pm Sat; M Spagna)

Local Life
Via Margutta

A narrow, cobbled lane lined with art studios, antique shops and ochre *palazzi*, **Via Margutta** (Map p58, C3; M Spagna) is picture-perfect Rome. It has long had an arty reputation and it was in the Valeria Moncada Gallery at No 54 that the futurists held their first meeting and Picasso met his wife Olga. More recently, Federico Fellini lived at No 110 until his death in 1993.

Eating

Babette INTERNATIONAL €€€

5 Map p58, B2

With its French-brasserie look, prime location and tranquil private courtyard, Babette is a real charmer. The seasonal menu does its part, too, offering sophisticated Italian fare alongside Argentinean steaks and French-inspired soufflés, flans and soups. At lunchtime, the buffet spread is excellent value, particularly on weekdays (€10 Tuesday to Friday, €25 Saturday and Sunday). Book for dinner. (✆06 321 15 59; www.babetteristorante.it; Via Margutta 1; meals €50-55; ⏱Tue-Sun; Ⓜ Flaminio or Spagna)

Al Gran Sasso TRATTORIA €€

6 Map p58, A2

The perfect lunchtime spot, this is a classic, dyed-in-the-wool trattoria serving filling portions of old-school country cooking. It's a relaxed place with a welcoming vibe, garish murals on the walls (strangely, often a good sign) and tasty, value-for-money food. The fried dishes are especially good and there's fresh fish on Tuesdays and Fridays. (✆06 321 48 83; www.trattoriaal gransasso.com; Via di Ripetta 32; meals €25; ⏱Sun-Fri; Ⓜ Flaminio)

Imàgo GASTRONOMIC €€€

7 Map p58, D4

Even in a city of great views, the panoramas from the Hassler Hotel's romantic rooftop restaurant are quite

---

Understand
La Passeggiata

One of the quintessential rituals of Roman life is the early evening *passeggiata* (promenade). Every evening, typically between 5pm and 8pm, locals of all ages pour onto the streets to hang out in the piazzas and parade up and down the main thoroughfares. They won't have a destination in mind because the *passeggiata* isn't about going anywhere, rather it's an occasion to see and be seen, to chat with mates, flirt, and eye people up. In eras past the *passeggiata* was the time for officially sanctioned courting, and parents would encourage their eligible daughters to don their finest clothes and put on a good performance. Still today, Romans like to dress up and show their colours, particularly at weekends when families, friends and lovers take to the streets en masse. For the best spectacle, head to Via del Corso and the streets around Piazza di Spagna.

special (request the corner table for the best vista), extending over a sea of roofs to the great dome of St Peter's Basilica. Complementing the views are the bold, mod-Italian creations of culinary star, chef Francesco Apreda. Book ahead. (☎06 6993 4726; www.imagorestaurant.com; Piazza della Trinità dei Monti 6; tasting menus €100-140; ⏰dinner; Ⓜ Spagna)

'Gusto MODERN ITALIAN €

8 Map p58, A3

This warehouse-style gastronomic complex, all exposed brickwork and industrial chic, is hugely popular with local lunchers who flock here to sit on the sunny terrace and pile into the bountiful midday buffet. The jumbo-sized Neapolitan pizzas are also a good bet, but the upmarket restaurant fare receives mixed reports. (☎06 322 62 73; Piazza Augusto Imperatore 9; lunch buffet from €9, pizzas from €7; 🚌Via del Corso)

Palatium TRADITIONAL ITALIAN €€

9 Map p58, C4

Drop those Valentino shopping bags and refuel at this sleek showcase for Lazio's bumper produce. Explore lesser-known local wines such as Aleatico, and dine on regional specialities such as *porchetta* (herbed spit-roasted pork) from Ariccia, artisanal cheeses, olives and salami. For nibbles, drop by for an early evening *aperitivo*. (☎06 6920 2132; Via Frattina 94; meals €40-45; ⏰11am-11pm Mon-Sat, closed Aug; Ⓜ Spagna)

Antica Enoteca TRADITIONAL ITALIAN €€

10 Map p58, C3

Local shoppers and shopkeepers pack this much-loved wine bar, which is full of frescoes and 19th-century trimmings. Plonk yourself at the long wood-and-brass counter and take your pick from 60 Italian drops by the glass; or plunge into the back room for soul-food staples such as pasta and polenta. (☎06 679 08 96; Via della Croce 76b; meals €40-45; ⏰noon-midnight; Ⓜ Spagna)

Margutta Ristorarte VEGETARIAN €€

11 Map p58, B2

Specialist vegetarian restaurants are as rare as free parking spaces in Rome, but this vibrant restaurant-gallery defiantly flies the flag for meat-free dining. Svelte design and bilingual staff pair perfectly with an impressive wine list and a wide-ranging menu of thoughtful dishes, many prepared with organic ingredients. Brunch is served daily, culminating in a wonderful weekend spread. (☎06 678 60 33; www.ilmargutta.it; Via Margutta 118; meals €45-50, weekend brunch €25, vegan menu €50; Ⓜ Flaminio or Spagna)

Local Life

Pastificio

For most of the day, **Pastificio** (Map p58, C3; Via della Croce; pasta dishes €4; ⏰1-3pm Mon-Sat; Ⓜ Spagna) goes about its business as a fresh pasta shop but at lunchtime it turns itself into the neighbourhood's budget diner. Locals pile in to fill up on the daily pasta dishes (there's a choice of two), eaten out of plastic bowls wherever there's room.

La Buca di Ripetta

TRADITIONAL ITALIAN €€

 12   Map p58, A2

A hit with local actors and directors, as well as passing tourists, La Buca has been part of the neighbourhood since the early 1900s. To a rustic-chic backdrop of shelved wine bottles and framed prints, diners are treated to creamy risottos, creative meat and fish dishes, and robust Roman fail-safes. Head in before 2pm to avoid the lunch crowds, and book for dinner. (☎06 321 93 91; www.labucadiripetta.com; Via di Ripetta 36; meals €45; Ⓜ Flaminio)

Osteria Margutta

MODERN ITALIAN €€€

13   Map p58, C3

Looking straight out of *Moulin Rouge* with its red velvet curtains and fancy fringed lampshades, Osteria Margutta has plaques on its chairs testifying

to the famous thespian bums they've supported. The menu mixes it up with classic Roman staples alongside more inventive dishes, homemade desserts and a top wine list. (☎06 323 10 25; www.osteriamargutta.it; Via Margutta 82; meals €65-70; ⏰Mon-Sat; Ⓜ Spagna)

Gina

CAFE €€

 14   Map p58, D3

Shop till you drop then stop by for a bite at white-on-white Gina, just around the corner from the Spanish Steps. This is where the Prada set come to flirt, gossip and nibble on club sandwiches and light lunches of panini, soups, bruschetta and fresh, inspired salads. Should romance spark, Villa Borghese picnic hampers (€40) are available for two. (Via San Sebastianello 7a; snacks €10-15; ⏰11am-8pm; Ⓜ Spagna)

Drinking

La Scena

BAR

 15   Map p58, A2

Fashionistas and style gurus congregate on this rakish lounge bar for their *aperitivo*. Part of the ravishing art deco Hotel Locarno near Piazza del Popolo, it's an inspiring spot for a sundowner with romantic corners, a shaded outdoor terrace, heavy cast-iron tables and a decadent Agatha Christie–era feel. (Via della Penna 22; Ⓜ Flaminio)

Caffè Greco

Stravinskij Bar at Hotel de Russie

BAR

16 🍸 Map p58, B1

With its lushly planted terraces, potted orange trees and just-love-to-please-you waiters, Hotel de Russie's ritzy courtyard bar oozes *dolce vita* style. Go ahead – order the smoky Lapsang martini, slip on some shades and scan the bar for checked-in stars. (Via del Babuino 9; ⏰9am-1am; Ⓜ Flaminio)

Caffè Greco

CAFE

17 🍸 Map p58, C4

Casanova, Goethe, Keats, Byron and Baudelaire were regulars at the legendary Greco, which has been clattering cups since 1760. It's an elegant marble-and-gilt cafe, a favourite with tour parties, but if you come in the early morning and sip at the bar, you'll avoid the worst of the crowds and the worst of the prices. (Via dei Condotti 86; ⏰9am-8pm; Ⓜ Spagna)

Canova Tadolini

CAFE

18 🍸 Map p58, B3

Although touristy, this is a unique, kitschy spot for an upmarket tea or glass of wine. In 1818 sculptor Canova signed a contract for the studio that agreed it would be forever preserved for sculpture. And almost two centuries on it's still stuffed with statues and great maquettes. (Via del Babuino 150a/b; ⏰9am-10.30pm Mon-Sat; Ⓜ Spagna)

Shopping

Eleonora
FASHION

19 🔒 Map p58, C3

Burst past the faux-trashy entrance and visit this Tridente hot spot for a classy selection of designer-ware, from the likes of Dolce & Gabbana, Fendi, Missoni, Marc Jacobs and Sergio Rossi. (Via del Babuino 97; ⏰10am-7.30pm Mon-Sat, 11am-7.30pm Sun; M Spagna)

Bomba
FASHION

20 🔒 Map p58, A2

Discerning Romans worship Cristina Bomba's high-quality knitwear and modish accessories. Her discreet boutique also showcases gowns, hats, jewellery and shoes by other designers and hosts the occasional art exhibition. (www.cristinabomba.com; Via dell'Oca 39-41; ⏰11am-7.30pm Tue-Sat, 3.30-7.30pm Mon; M Flaminio)

Alinari
ANTIQUES, BOOKSTORE

21 🔒 Map p58, C3

Head to the world's oldest photographic archive for evocative prints and postcards of Rome and Italy by the Alinari brothers, who were 19th-century Florentine photographers. A smattering of chunky photography tomes will keep your coffee table humming. (Via Alibert 16; M Spagna)

Fausto Santini
SHOES

22 🔒 Map p58, C4

God to fashionable feet, Fausto Santini is Rome's best-known shoe designer, famous for his show-stopping creations and gorgeous bags in obscenely soft leather. Colours are beautiful and quality impeccable. (www.faustosantini .com; Via Frattina 120; ⏰11am-7.30pm Mon, 10am-7.30pm Tue-Sat, 11am-2pm & 3-7pm Sun; M Spagna)

Gente
FASHION

23 🔒 Map p58, B2

Gente stocks superlative Italian and foreign labels, including Prada, Paul Smith and Tom Ford. Female fashion junkies can get their fix down the street at No 81. Those with more style than savings should pop into Outlet Gente (p153) for remainders and last-season reductions. (Via del Babuino 185; ⏰3.30-7.30pm Mon, 10.30am-7.30pm Tue-Sat, noon-7.30pm Sun; M Flaminio or Spagna)

Fabriano
STATIONERY

24 🔒 Map p58, B2

Fabriano makes stationery sexy with its collection of brightly coloured diaries, funky notebooks and tan leather sleeves for iPhones and iPads. Enlightened extras include quirky paper jewellery made by local designers and stylish paper-thin wallets. (www. fabrianoboutique.com; Via del Babuino 173; ⏰10am-8pm daily; M Flaminio or Spagna)

Buccone
FOOD, WINE

25 Map p58, A2

Salivate over soaring vintage shelves crammed with foodie-fabulous oils, vinegars, sauces, pastas, regional Italian *biscotti* (biscuits) and wines from Sicily to South Australia. Come at lunch (12.30pm to 3pm) and you can also grab a plate of pasta or salad. Dinner is also served from 7.30pm to 10.30pm Friday and Saturday. (www .enotecabuccone.com; Via di Ripetta 19-20; ⊙9am-8.30pm Mon-Thu, to 11.30pm Fri & Sat; MFlaminio)

Furla
ACCESSORIES

26 Map p58, D3

Simple, good-quality bags in soft leather and a brilliant array of colours are why the hand-bagging hordes keep flocking to Furla. It also does a popular line in fashion-savvy accessories, wallets, key rings and sunglasses. (www.furla.com; Piazza di Spagna 22; ⊙10am-8pm Mon-Sat, 10.30am-8pm Sun; MSpagna)

Louis Vuitton
FASHION

27 Map p58, C4

Forget bags and the brand's other sought-after accessories, the star turn here is the eye-catching, plasma-screen staircase. Based on a concept by New York–based architect Peter Marino (and looking like it's straight off a Madonna concert set), this visual tour de force transforms itself from psychedelic snake to technicolour torrent in seconds. (www.louisvuitton.com; Via dei Condotti 13; ⊙10am-7.30pm Mon-Sat, 11am-7.30pm Sun; MSpagna)

Sermoneta
ACCESSORIES

28 Map p58, D4

At Rome's most famous glove-seller choose from a kaleidoscopic range of quality leather and suede gloves with linings in silk and cashmere. An expert assistant will size up your hand in a glance – just don't expect them to smile. (www.sermonetagloves.com; Piazza di Spagna 61; ⊙9.30am-8pm Mon-Sat, 10am-7pm Sun; MSpagna)

Explore

Trevi & the Quirinale

Home to *that* fountain, Trevi's lively medieval streets feel a bit like a circus with their camcorder crowds and endless souvenir shops. But head up the Quirinale hill and the atmosphere changes as you come face to face with the presidential Palazzo del Quirinale and a number of distinguished baroque churches. Other hot spots include Palazzo Barberini and Saturday-only Palazzo e Galleria Colonna.

The Sights in a Day

☀ Get the day off to a sweet start with breakfast at the Sicilian cafe **Dagnino** (p76). From there, it's a short walk up to the **Chiesa di Santa Maria della Vittoria** (p71) and an awe-inspiring Bernini masterpiece. For a further fill of baroque pomp and Renaissance revelations head to the **Galleria Nazionale d'Arte Antica – Palazzo Barberini** (p71), a superb art gallery housed in one of Rome's great aristocratic *palazzi* (mansions). Next, lunch at **Colline Emiliane** (p75).

☀ Fed and watered, head uphill to the Quirinale. Check out Borromini's **Chiesa di San Carlo alle Quattro Fontane** (p72) and push on to Piazza del Quirinale and the majestic **Palazzo del Quirinale** (p71). If there's an exhibition on, stop at the **Scuderie Papali al Quirinale** (p72), otherwise duck down the steps near the piazza and follow on to the **Trevi Fountain** (detail pictured left; p68). Throw your coins away and then treat yourself to an ice cream from **Il Gelato di San Crispino** (p75).

☾ Wind up the day with some late-night jazz tunes at **Gregory's** (p77).

 Top Sights

Trevi Fountain (p68)

💜 **Best of Rome**

Museums

Galleria Nazionale d'Arte Antica – Palazzo Barberini (p71)

Palazzo e Galleria Colonna (p71)

Eating

Colline Emiliane (p75)

Il Gelato di San Crispino (p75)

Da Michele (p75)

Culture

Gregory's (p77)

Scuderie Papali al Quirinale (p72)

Gagosian Gallery (p73)

Architecture

Chiesa di San Carlo alle Quattro Fontane (p72)

Getting There

Ⓜ Metro Get off at Barberini (line A) for the Trevi Fountain, Quirinale and Via Vittorio Veneto.

🚌 Bus Take bus 40, 64 or H for Via Nazionale, from where you can access the Quirinale; buses 52 and 53 stop at Piazza Barberini, near the metro station.

Top Sights
Trevi Fountain

The Fontana di Trevi, immortalised by Anita Ekberg's dip in *La Dolce Vita*, is Rome's largest and
most famous fountain. A theatrical ensemble of
mythical figures, wild horses and cascading rock
falls, it takes up the entire side of 17th-century
Palazzo Poli. Completed in 1762, it's named Trevi
in reference to the *tre vie* (three roads) that con-
verge on it. The fountain is about to undergo a
€2.2m 20-month restoration funded by the Fendi
fashion house.

◉ Map p70, A3

Piazza di Trevi

Ⓜ Barberini

Don't Miss

Neptune & His Seahorses

Designed by Nicola Salvi in 1732, the fountain depicts Neptune, the god of the sea, in a shell-shaped chariot being led by Tritons and two seahorses – one wild, one docile – representing the moods of the sea. In the niche to the left of Neptune, a statue represents Abundance; to the right is Salubrity.

Throwing Your Coin In

The famous tradition is to stand with your back to the fountain and toss a coin over your shoulder into the water, thus ensuring your return to the Eternal City. According to the same tradition, if you throw in a second coin you'll fall in love with an Italian, and a third will have you marrying him or her.

On an average day about €3000 is thrown into the Trevi Fountain. This is collected daily and given to the Catholic charity Caritas, but in 2002 scandal erupted when it was discovered that an unemployed man calling himself D'Artagnan had been helping himself for 34 years. In fact, until legislation was recently passed, the only legal obstacle to removing the coins was a law prohibiting entering the fountain.

The Asso di Coppe

Look on the wall to the right of the fountain and you'll see a strange conical statue. This is the *Assso di coppe* (Ace of Cups) that Nicola Salvi placed there to block the view of a busybody barber who criticised the fountain design during construction.

☑ Top Tips

▶ Avoid the crowds and come at the crack of dawn.

▶ Have some coins ready to throw in.

▶ Costumed centurions hang around the fountain volunteering to pose with you for your photos. They expect payment.

▶ The fountain's dazzling white stone photographs best in soft late-afternoon light.

▶ Come after dark to see the fountain magically illuminated.

✘ Take a Break

For a quick fuel stop or an easy takeaway lunch, search out Da Michele (p75) and grab a slice of pizza. If you're in the mood for ice cream, nearby Il Gelato di San Crispino (p75) serves some of the best in town.

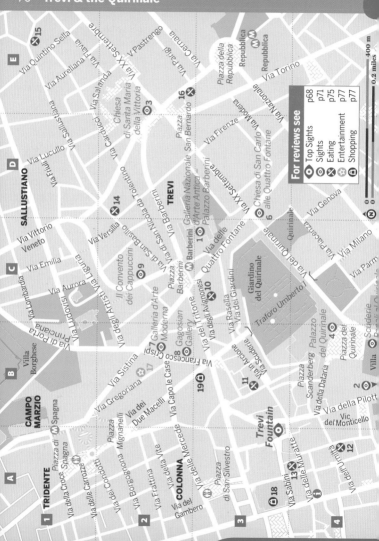

TRIDENTE

CAMPO MARZIO

SALLUSTIANO

COLONNA

TREVI

Villa Borghese

Piazza di Spagna

Piazza Mignanelli

Piazza di San Silvestro

Chiesa di Santa Maria della Vittoria

Piazza della Repubblica

Repubblica

Chiesa di San Carlo alle Quattro Fontane

Galleria Nazionale d'Arte Antica – Palazzo Barberini

Piazza Barberini

Il Convento dei Cappuccini

Galleria d'Arte Moderna

Gagosian Gallery

Giardino del Quirinale

Traforo Umberto I

Palazzo del Quirinale

Piazza del Quirinale

Piazza Scanderberg

Piazza della Dataria

Vic del Monticello

Trevi Fountain

Via Quintino Sella

Via XX Settembre

Via La Fava

Via Aureliana

Via Salandra

V Pastrengo

Via Parigi

Via Cernaia

Via Luciano

Via Sallustiana

Via di Porta Pinciana

Via Ludovisi

Via degli Artisti

Via Lombardia

Via Emilia

Via Aurora

Via Liguria

Via Sistina

Via Gregoriana

Via Vittorio Veneto

Via Versilla

Via di San Basilio

Via San Nicola da Tolentino

Via di Santa Maria della Vittoria

Via Barberini

Via delle Quattro Fontane

Via delle Quattro Fontane

Via XX Settembre

Via Firenze

Via Moderna

Via Nazionale

Via Torino

Via Genova

Via Milano

Via Parm

Via Piacenza

Via del Quirinale

Via del Quirinale

Via della Pilott

Via Rasella

Via dei Giardini

Via del Tritone

Via Francesco Crispi

Via degli Avignonesi

Via del Tritone

Via in Arcione

Via della Stamperia

Via delle Vergini

Via del Lavatore

Via delle Muratte

Via Sabini

Via dell'Umiltà

Via delle Murate

Via della Vite

Via Frattina

Via del Gambero

Via della Mercede

Via Capo le Case

Via dei Due Macelli

Via Borgognona

Via dei Condotti

Via delle Carrozze

Via della Croce

Piazza di Spagna

Via Frattina

Scuderie

Villa

15

3

16

14

9

1

10

6

7

8

17

19

11

4

2

18

13

12

For reviews see	
Top Sights	p68
Sights	p71
Eating	p75
Entertainment	p77
Shopping	p77

0   400 m
0   0.2 miles

Sights

Galleria Nazionale d'Arte Antica – Palazzo Barberini
GALLERY

1 Map p70, C3

A who's who of baroque architects created this magnificent 17th-century palace, now home to a sumptuous collection of Renaissance and baroque art. Take in works by Caravaggio, Raphael, El Greco, Tintoretto, Bronzino and Hans Holbein, and, for that ultimate rush, soak up Pietro da Cortona's almighty ceiling fresco, *Trionfo della divina provvidenza* (Triumph of Divine Providence; 1632–39) in the main salon. (www.galleriaborghese.it; Via delle Quattro Fontane 13; adult/reduced €7/3.50; ☺8.30am-7pm Tue-Sun; Ⓜ Barberini)

Palazzo e Galleria Colonna
GALLERY

2 Map p70, B4

On Saturday mornings, the aristocratic Colonna clan allows commoners into its opulent 17th-century gallery to browse its family art collection. Loud, glorious ceiling frescoes record the family's virtuous deeds, while below them hang canvases by artistic greats, including Bronzino, Veronese, Salvatore Rosa and Annibale Carracci, whose humble *Bean Eater* is the crowd favourite. (www.galleriacolonna.it; Via della Pilotta 17; adult/reduced €12/10; ☺9am-1.15pm Sat, closed Aug; 🚊 Via IV Novembre)

Chiesa di Santa Maria della Vittoria
CHURCH

3 Map p70, E2

This modest baroque church is an unlikely setting for one of the great works of European art. Bernini's sexually charged *Santa Teresa traffita dall'amore di dio* (Ecstasy of St Teresa) depicts the Spanish saint floating in ecstasy on a cloud while a teasing angel pierces her with a golden arrow. A mesmerising work, it's best viewed in sensual afternoon light. (Via XX Settembre 17; ☺7am-noon & 3.30-7pm; Ⓜ Repubblica)

Palazzo del Quirinale
PALAZZO

4 Map p70, B4

Overlooking Piazza del Quirinale, this immense palace is the residence of Italy's head of state, the Presidente della Repubblica. For much of its lifetime it was the pope's summer palace but in 1870 he reluctantly gave it up

Ⓠ Local Life
Sunsets on the Quirinale

One of the best places to catch a memorable Roman view is **Piazza del Quirinale** (Map p70, B4) in front of the presidential palace. As the sun dips and the sky takes on a golden, fiery hue you can gaze over a sea of rooftops to the distant dome of St Peter's Basilica (Basilica di San Pietro).

NEIL SETCHFIELD/LONELY PLANET IMAGES ©

Ceiling fresco, Galleria Nazionale d'Arte Antica – Palazzo Barberini (p71)

to Italy's new king. Domenico Fontana designed the main facade, Carlo Maderno the chapel, and Bernini the wing running the length of the street. (www .quirinale.it; Piazza del Quirinale; admission €5; ⊘8am-noon Sun mid-Sep–Jun; 🚌Via Nazionale)

Scuderie Papali al Quirinale
GALLERY

5 ◎ Map p70, B4

Across the piazza from the Palazzo del Quirinale is this slick gallery and exhibition centre. Occupying the palace's former stables, it was fashioned by Italian architect Gae Aulenti (of Musée d'Orsay fame) in the late 1990s and now hosts major art exhibitions.

Admission prices vary and opening hours depend on exhibitions. (www .scuderiequirinale.it; Via XXIV Maggio 16; 🚌Via Nazionale)

Chiesa di San Carlo alle Quattro Fontane
CHURCH

6 ◎ Map p70, D3

It might not look it, with its filthy facade and unappealing location, but Borromini's first church is a masterpiece of Roman baroque. Completed in 1641, it bears all the hallmarks of his tormented genius, from the play of convex and concave surfaces to its incredible honeycomb dome, which seems to float above your head (the secret is in the cunningly hidden windows). (Via del Quirinale 23; ☉10am-1pm & 3-6pm Mon-Fri, 10am-1pm Sat, noon-1pm Sun; Ⓜ Barberini)

Galleria d'Arte Moderna
GALLERY

7 Map p70, B2

A welcome addition to Rome's modern art scene, this bright, airy gallery opened in November 2011. The collection, housed in a restored 18th-century convent, comprises sculpture, paintings, drawings and prints, with some forceful portraits by Giacomo Balla, a section dedicated to visions of Rome, and a voluptuous sculpture of Cleopatra by Gerolamo Masini. (www.galleriaartemodernaroma.it; Via Francesco Crispi 24; adult/reduced €6.50/5.50; ☉10am-6pm Tue-Sun; Ⓜ Barberini)

Gagosian Gallery
GALLERY

8 Map p70, B2

Since it opened in 2007, the Rome branch of Larry Gagosian's contemporary art empire has hosted the big names of modern art: Cy Twombly, Damien Hirst, Lawrence Weiner and Walter De Maria, to name a few. The gallery occupies a stylishly converted 1920s bank, complete with a theatrical neoclassical facade. (www.gagosian.com; Via Francesco Crispi 16; admission free; ☉10.30am-7pm Tue-Sat; Ⓜ Barberini)

Understand
Bernini & Borromini, Rome's Baroque Rivals

Born within a year of each other, the two giants of Roman baroque hated each other with a vengeance. While Gian Lorenzo Bernini (1598–1680) was an ebullient, urbane player (he seduced the pope's niece to nab the commission for the Fontana dei Quattro Fiumi), Francesco Borromini (1599–1677) was neurotic, reclusive and tortured.

They worked together on St Peter's Basilica and Palazzo Barberini but for most of their careers they competed for commissions and public acclaim. Bernini flourished under Pope Urban VIII (r 1623–44) and Borromini under his successor Innocent X (r 1644–55), but all the while their loathing simmered. Borromini sniffed at Bernini's lack of architectural training while Bernini claimed that Borromini 'had been sent to destroy architecture'.

Of the two, Bernini is generally reckoned to have had the better of the rivalry. His genius was rarely questioned and when he died he was widely regarded as one of Europe's greatest artists. Borromini struggled to win popular and critical support and after a life of depression committed suicide in 1677.

Understand

Rome in Film

Rome has long been a favourite city for film-makers. Over the years, its historic monuments and seductive piazzas have appeared in everything from neorealist tear-jerkers to arthouse classics, modern thrillers and sugar-coated rom-coms. And with Woody Allen's *To Rome with Love* hitting screens in 2012, this long-standing love affair shows no signs of burning out.

Neorealism in the Suburbs

Roberto Rossellini's 1945 masterpiece *Roma Città Aperta* (Rome Open City) was made on location in Rome's battered postwar streets. Filmed in the working-class Prenestina district, it paved the way for films by Vittorio De Sica and Pier Paolo Pasolini, whose *Accattone* (1961) was partly set in the Pigneto neighbourhood (p92).

Scoot Around the Sights

Starring Gregory Peck and Audrey Hepburn, the classic rom-com *Roman Holiday* (1953) presents a more traditional portrait of Rome, featuring sights such as the Colosseum (Colosseo; p24), Roman Forum (Foro Romano; p26) and Bocca della Verità (p33).

Federico Fellini also made use of Rome's attributes. Most famously, in *La Dolce Vita* (1960), he had Anita Ekberg splashing in the Trevi Fountain (actually a specially built reconstruction; p68), and losing her hat on the dome of St Peter's Basilica (p138).

Pantheon & Piazzas

The Pantheon (p38) has appeared in everything from Peter Greenaway's *Belly of an Architect* (1987) to *Angels and Demons* (2009), which bounces between various locations, including the Chiesa di Santa Maria del Popolo (p59) and Piazza Navona (p44), which also gets the postcard treatment in *Eat, Pray, Love* (2010).

Rome's piazzas are a sure thing for directors requiring atmosphere. In *The Talented Mr Ripley* (1999), Piazza di Spagna (p57) provides a moneyed setting for the film's glossy characters. Similarly, Piazza Santa Maria in Trastevere (p125) screams charm in *Barney's Version* (2010).

Il Convento dei Cappuccini
MUSEUM

9 Map p70, C2

This convent has an interesting multi-media museum telling the story of the Capuchin order of monks. But the main act is the ghoulish **Capuchin cemetery** where the bones of 4000 monks have been revamped into everything from lanterns to flouncy fleurs-de-lis. There's even a child-sized skeleton holding the scales of justice and scythe of death. (Via Vittorio Veneto 27; adult/reduced €6/4; ⊙9am-7pm daily; M Barberini)

Eating

Colline Emiliane
REGIONAL ITALIAN €€

10 Map p70, C3

This warm, elegant restaurant flies the flag for Emilia-Romagna, the Italian region that gave the world Parmesan, balsamic vinegar, Bolognese sauce and Parma ham. So expect lush creamy sauces, robust meat dishes and scrumptious homemade pastas such as *tortelli di zucca* (pockets of pasta-like ravioli stuffed with pumpkin). Reservations are highly recommended. (☏06 481 75 38; Via degli Avignonesi 22; meals €45; ⊙lunch & dinner Tue-Sat, lunch Sun, closed Aug; M Barberini)

Il Gelato di San Crispino
GELATERIA €

11 Map p70, B3

A serious contender for the title of Rome's best gelateria. The ice cream, which is religiously stored under stainless steel lids, is made with seasonal, strictly natural ingredients resulting in unforgettable flavours such as *fichi secci* (dried figs), *miele* (honey) and *basilico* (basil). Just don't expect a cone, it's tubs only here (cones would detract from the taste). (Via della Panetteria 42; ⊙noon-12.30am Mon, Wed, Thu & Sun, 11am-1.30am Fri & Sat; M Barberini)

Da Michele
PIZZA AL TAGLIO €

12 Map p70, A4

There are a lot of takeaways in the lanes and alleys around the Trevi Fountain, but few serve pizza as good as this handy bolthole. It's not that Da Michele does fancy toppings or gourmet combos, it's just that the old favourites it serves taste so perfectly right. Take the potato and sausage pizza – the topping is fresh and moist and the base light, dry and crispy, just as it should be. (Via dell'Umiltà 31; pizza slices €3; ⊙8am-5pm Mon-Fri, to 8pm summer; 🚌Via del Corso)

Al Moro

TRADITIONAL ITALIAN €€€

13 Map p70, A4

A neighbourhood institution, this one-time Fellini haunt feels like a step back in time with its picture-gallery dining rooms, Liberty wall lamps and cantankerous buttoned-up waiters. The old-school menu stays in theme, with handmade pastas, minestrones, grilled and boiled meats and home-made cakes for pud. (☑06 678 34 96; www.ristorantealmororoma.com; Vicolo delle Bollette 13; meals €50-60; ☺Mon-Sat; ☑Via del Corso)

Moma

MODERN ITALIAN €€€

14 Map p70, D2

Paging London with its angular grey-black minimalism and sexed-up metro style, Moma splits itself in two: there's a downstairs bar for stand-up espresso and ab-fab nibbles, and an upstairs dining room for adventurous mod-Med creations. Book for dinner. (☑06 4201 1798; Via San Basilio 42; meals €60; ☺7am-11pm Mon-Sat; Ⓜ Barberini)

Cantina Cantarini

TRATTORIA €€

15 Map p70, E1

Leave the tourist hordes behind as you hike out to this salt-of-the-earth trattoria that has been feeding locals for more than a century. In that time little has changed and the focus is still on simple, robust dishes from the Lazio and Le Marche regions, served in warm, woody surroundings. Get

in early or queue. (☑06 48 55 28; Piazza Sallustio 12; meals €30; ☺closed Sun & Aug; ☑Via XX Settembre)

Dagnino

PASTRIES & CAKES €

16 Map p70, E2

Sweet tooths cram this busy cafe-cum-*pasticceria* (pastry shop) for sublime Sicilian treats, from heavenly *cannoli* and ice-cream brioche to velvety

---

Understand
Ice Cream

Eating gelato is as much a part of Roman life as traffic jams. And with good reason, as the city boasts some fantastic artisanal gelaterie.

No one is quite sure where or when ice cream originated, but it's said that Nero used to snack on snow mixed with fruit pulp and honey, and that the Arabs introduced techniques for making sorbets when they colonised Sicily in the 9th century. Whatever. The fact remains that Italian ice cream is superb. The best is always made from fresh, seasonal ingredients – so no strawberry in winter – sourced from top-quality producers. And don't be fooled by appearances. Good-quality gelato is not necessarily the prettiest on show, so top-notch pistachio ice cream is a dull ochre-green colour rather than bright, vibrant green. Ditto, the banana: bright yellow equals bad, grey is good.

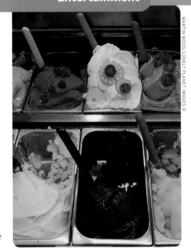

marzipan fruits. You can sit down to a full lunch but the offerings tend to be hit and miss and you're better off standing and snacking on *arancini* (deep-fried rice balls). (Galleria Esedra, Via Vittorio Emanuele Orlando; cannoli €2.60, meals €15-20; ⏱7am-11pm; Ⓜ Repubblica)

Entertainment

Gregory's   LIVE MUSIC

17 ⭐ Map p70, B2

This husky, soulful jazz den is a popular hang-out for Roman musicians and a good bet for top local sax. Unwind in the downstairs bar, then move upstairs and unwind some more to slinky live jazz. (📞06 679 63 86; www.gregorysjazz.com; Via Gregoriana 54a; ⏱7pm-2am Tue-Sun Sep-Jun; Ⓜ Barberini or Spagna)

Shopping

Galleria Alberto Sordi   SHOPPING CENTRE

18 🔒 Map p70, A3

Film buffs may recall this elegant stained-glass arcade from Alberto Sordi's 1973 film classic, *Polvere di stelle* (Stardust). The film starred Rome's favourite actor, for whom the gallery was renamed in 2003. Retail protagonists include Calvin Klein

Gelati

Jeans, Zara, TJ Trussardi Jeans and Feltrinelli, and there's a chic cafe for cinematic posing. (Piazza Colonna; ⏱10am-10pm; 🚌 Via del Corso)

Victory   FASHION

19 🔒 Map p70, B3

Victory, a discreet store near Piazza di Spagna, stocks male wardrobe winners such as Dondup jeans, Gaetano Navarra shirts and Herno coats. Clued-up ladies can get their fix across the street at No 103–4. (Via dei Due Macelli 32; ⏱10am-8pm Mon-Sat, noon-7.30pm Sun; Ⓜ Barberini)

Explore

Monti & Esquilino

With its village vibe and sloping, cobbled lanes, Monti is one of Rome's coolest quarters. In ancient times it was the city's red-light district but it now plays host to a colourful cast of studios, boutiques, bars and restaurants. Rising to the east, cosmopolitan Esquilino (Esquiline) boasts some amazing churches, one of Rome's best museums, and the transport hub Stazione Termini.

The Sights in a Day

☀ Leave the choking chaos of Termini behind as you enter the hushed halls of the **Museo Nazionale Romano: Palazzo Massimo alle Terme** (p80), one of Rome's unsung heroes. Lose yourself among the sculpture and frescoes before heading over to the **Basilica di Santa Maria Maggiore** (interior detail pictured left; p84) and nearby **Chiesa di Santa Prassede** (p84), famous for its glorious Byzantine mosaics. After so much worthy art, treat yourself to lunch at **Trattoria Monti** (p86).

☀ First stop on the afternoon agenda (but make it after 3pm) is the **Basilica di San Pietro in Vincoli** (p84), boasting a resident Michelangelo. Afterwards, push on to Monti to explore the boutiques and ateliers of **Via del Boschetto** (p91). From the top of the street, make for **Palazzo delle Esposizioni** (p85) to check out an exhibition.

☾ Spend the evening in the attractive confines of Monti. Start with dinner at **L'Asino d'Oro** (p87), then take your pick from the area's many bars and cafes – **Ai Tre Scalini** (p88) is always a popular choice.

 Top Sights

Museo Nazionale Romano: Palazzo Massimo alle Terme (p80)

💜 **Best of Rome**

Art

Museo Nazionale Romano: Palazzo Massimo alle Terme (p80)

Chiesa di Santa Prassede (p84)

Basilica di Santa Maria Maggiore (p84)

Eating

Trattoria Monti (p86)

Agata e Romeo (p87)

Palazzo del Freddo di Giovanni Fassi (p87)

Getting There

Ⓜ **Metro** For Monti, get off at Cavour on line B. Termini (lines A & B), Castro Pretorio (line B) and Vittorio Emanuele (line A) are useful for Esquilino.

🚌 **Bus** Termini is the city's main bus hub, with connections to all corners of the city. Monti is accessible via buses that stop on Via Nazionale or Via Cavour.

Top Sights
Museo Nazionale Romano: Palazzo Massimo alle Terme

Every day, thousands of tourists, commuters and passers-by hurry past this towering Renaissance *palazzo* (mansion) without giving it a second glance. They don't know what they're missing. For this is one of Rome's great museums, an oft-overlooked treasure trove of classical art. The sculpture is truly impressive but what really takes the breath away is the collection of vibrantly coloured ancient frescoes and mosaics.

👁 Map p82, D2

Largo di Villa Peretti 1

adult/reduced incl Crypta Balbi, Palazzo Altemps & Terme di Diocleziano €7/3.50, plus possible €3 exhibition supplement

🕑 9am-7.45pm Tue-Sun

🚇 M Termini

Mosaic floor detail

Don't Miss

Ground Floor

The ground floor is dedicated to some really wonderful sculpture. Show-stoppers include the 5th-century-BC *Niobide dagli horti sallustiani* (Niobide from the Gardens of Sallust), which movingly depicts a young woman trying to pull an arrow out of her back, and the *Pugile* (Boxer), a 4th-century-BC Greek bronze of a resting boxer.

1st Floor

Upstairs, the sculptural show continues. Look out for *Il discobolo* (Discuss Thrower), a muscular and anatomically accurate 2nd-century copy of an ancient Greek work. Another admirable body belongs to the delicate and graceful *Ermafrodite dormiente* (Sleeping Hermaphrodite).

Frescoes & Mosaics

On the 2nd floor you'll find the museum's thrilling exhibition of ancient mosaics and frescoes. These vibrantly coloured panels were originally used as interior decoration in upmarket villas and are displayed in rooms that have been arranged to reflect the layout of the villas. There are intimate *cubicula* (bedroom) frescoes focusing on nature, mythology, domestic life and sensuality, and delicate landscape paintings from the winter *triclinium* (dining room).

Villa Livia Frescoes

The museum's crowning glory is this room of frescoes (dating from 30 to 20 BC) from Villa Livia, one of the homes of Augustus' wife Livia Drusilla. The paintings, which originally decorated a summer *triclinium*, cover an entire room, and depict a realistic yet paradisiacal garden full of roses, pomegranates, irises and poppies under a deep blue sky.

☑ **Top Tips**

▸ Head downstairs for Rome's largest coin collection.

▸ Remember that your ticket is valid for three days and provides admission to the other three sites of the Museo Nazionale Romano.

▸ The museum often stages excellent temporary exhibitions. If there's one on, you'll have to pay a €3 supplement on top of the regular ticket price.

✕ **Take a Break**

Revive sagging energy levels with a sugar fix from the historic Pasticceria Regoli (p88). Alternatively, drop into Panella L'Arte del Pane (p87) for a coffee and gourmet snack.

BY PHOTO ALAMY ©

E

Viale Enrico de Nicola

F

Via dei Mille
Via Magenta
Via Marghera

G

Via Palestro

H

N 0 ——— 200 m
0 ——— 0.1 miles

1

Piazza dei Cinquecento
P

Via Milazzo

Via di Castro Pretorio

Viale del Castro Pretoriano

Transport Information Booth
Main Bus Station
M
Termini

Via Marsala

Viale P Gobetti

2

Stazione Termini

Via Amendola

Via Gioberti
Via Filippo Turati

Tourist Information Point

3

Piazza Manfredo Fanti

Via Farini

Piazza Santa Maria Maggiore

Via Cattaneo
Via Rattazzi
Via Napoleone III
Via Principe Amedeo
Via A Cappellini

Via Giolitti

Via Mamiani

4

10
8
Via Carlo Alberto

Via Merulana

Largo Brancaccio
Via dello Statuto

5
Museo Nazionale d'Arte Orientale
11

Via Leopardi
Via Ferruccio
Via Buonarroti

Piazza Vittorio Emanuele II
Vittorio Emanuele
M

Via Ricasoli
Via Lamarmora
Via Principe Umberto
Via Giolitti

Via Principe Eugenio

5

21

12

ESQUILINO

For reviews see

◎	Top Sights	p80
◎	Sights	p84
✕	Eating	p86
🍷	Drinking	p88
★	Entertainment	p89
🛍	Shopping	p90

Sights

Basilica di San Pietro in Vincoli
CHURCH

1 ⊙ Map p82, B5

Beneath the altar of this 5th-century church sit the chains used to bind St Peter. According to legend, the chains miraculously rejoined after returning to Rome from Constantinople in two pieces. Nearby, Pope Julius II's monumental unfinished tomb is centred on Michelangelo's *Moses*, whose horns resulted when the Hebrew word for 'radiant' was mistranslated as 'horned'. (Piazza di San Pietro in Vincoli 4a; ⊙8am-12.30pm & 3-6pm, to 7pm summer; MCavour)

Basilica di Santa Maria Maggiore
CHURCH

2 ⊙ Map p82, D3

One of Rome's patriarchal basilicas, this landmark building has been much altered since it was built in the 5th century. Its bell tower, Rome's highest at 75m, is 14th-century Romanesque; the facade is 18th-century baroque; the Cosmati marble floor harks back to the 12th century; and the gilded ceiling is 15th century. Particularly spectacular are the 5th-century mosaics in the triumphal arch and nave. (Piazza Santa Maria Maggiore; ⊙7am-7pm; 🚇Piazza Santa Maria Maggiore)

Chiesa di Santa Prassede
CHURCH

3 ⊙ Map p82, D4

Humble Santa Prassede will blow you away with its dazzling 9th-century mosaics, whipped up by Byzantium artists brought in especially by Pope Paschal I. Swoon over the mosaics on the triumphal arch and apse, before hitting the jackpot in the extravagant Cappella di San Zenone (where you'll also find a piece of the column that Christ was tied to when flogged). (Via Santa Prassede 9a; ⊙7.30am-noon & 4-6.30pm; 🚇Piazza Santa Maria Maggiore)

Museo Nazionale Romano: Terme di Diocleziano
MUSEUM

4 ⊙ Map p82, D1

The 3rd-century Diocletian Baths were ancient Rome's largest, covering about 13 hectares and accommodating up to 3000 punters. Nowadays, the museum houses a famed collection of ancient epigraphs as well as a selection of tomb artefacts dating from the 9th to 11th centuries BC. Outside, classical sarcophagi, headless statues and huge animal heads line the Michelangelo-designed cloister. (Viale Enrico de Nicola 78; adult/reduced incl Crypta Balbi, Palazzo Altemps & Palazzo Massimo alle Terme €7/3.50, plus possible €3 exhibition supplement; ⊙9am-7.45pm Tue-Sun; 🚇MTermini)

Museo Nazionale d'Arte Orientale

MUSEUM

5 ⊙ Map p82, E5

Swap continents at Rome's little-known but impressive National Museum of Oriental Art. Set in 19th-century Palazzo Brancaccio, its collection of near- and far-eastern treasures includes carved ancient Afghani marble, richly hued Kubachi ceramics, painted Tibetan fans from the 11th to 18th centuries, and intricate Nepalese textiles. English-language information is wanting, but the pieces speak for themselves. (www.museorientale.beniculturali.it; Via Merulana 248; adult/reduced €6/3; ⊙9am-2pm Tue, Wed & Fri, to 7.30pm Thu, Sat & Sun; M Vittorio Emanuele)

Palazzo delle Esposizioni

GALLERY

6 ⊙ Map p82, A2

Built in 1882, and subsequently used as HQ for the Italian Communist Party and a mess hall for allied servicemen, this huge neoclassical cultural centre hosts blockbuster exhibitions as well as multimedia events, concerts, film screenings and conferences. Along with cathedral-scale exhibition spaces it also has a bookshop, cafe and top-notch restaurant. Opening hours depend on the exhibition. (www.palazzoesposizioni.it; Via Nazionale 194; ⊙10am-8pm Tue-Thu & Sun, to 10.30pm Fri & Sat ; 🚌 Via Nazionale)

Understand
Legend of the Magic Door

Porticoed **Piazza Vittorio Emanuele II** (Map p82, F5) is Rome's largest square (Piazza San Pietro is in the Vatican, so it doesn't count). Apart from the cheap and cheerful shops that surround it, the piazza's main interest lies in the pocket of ruins in the northeast corner of the fenced-off central section. Here, you'll see a mysterious limestone doorway covered in cabbalistic symbols and guarded by two monstrous Egyptian demigods. This is the **Porta Magica**, a door that once led to the private gardens of Villa Palombara, which stood here until the late 19th century.

According to legend, the villa's occult-loving owner, the Marquis Palombara, had sponsored the experiments of a young necromancer named Giuseppe Francesco Borri, who was set on discovering the legendary philosopher's stone (which turns matter into gold). But Borri vanished one day, leaving behind a pile of papers inscribed with secret formulae that the marquis hoped would unlock the magic formula. When even the best alchemists were left scratching their heads, Palombara engraved the symbols into the doorway, hoping that an expert would one day see them and finally crack the code.

PAOLO CORDELLI/LONELY PLANET IMAGES ©

Basilica di San Pietro in Vincoli (p84)

Piazza della Repubblica

PIAZZA

7 ⊙ Map p82, C1

Flanked by grand neoclassical colonnades, this landmark piazza was laid out in the late 19th century, shortly after Rome was made Italy's capital. It follows the lines of the semicircular *exedra* (benched portico) of the Diocletian Baths complex and was originally known as Piazza Esedra. In the centre, the **Fontana delle Naiadi** depicts four water nymphs surrounding the central figure of Glaucus wrestling a fish. (Ⓜ Repubblica)

Eating
Trattoria Monti

REGIONAL ITALIAN €€

8 ✕ Map p82, E4

Loved by locals and visitors alike, this intimate, arched restaurant – it's a trattoria in name only – is run by the charming Camerucci family. The reason for its popularity is its top-notch regional cooking from Le Marche (a hilly Apennine region on Italy's Adriatic coast). Expect exemplary game stews, pungent truffles and *pecorino di fossa* (sheep's cheese aged in caves), as well as wonderful fried starters such as *olive ascolane* (meat-stuffed olives). Book for dinner. (✆ 06 446 65

73; Via di San Vito 13a; meals €45; ⏱lunch & dinner Tue-Sat, lunch Sun; Ⓜ Vittorio Emanuele)

L'Asino d'Oro
MODERN ITALIAN €€

9 ✖️ Map p82, A3

This smart, inviting restaurant has been transplanted from Orvieto, and its Umbrian origins resonate in chef Lucio Sforza's exceptional cooking. The meat dishes are superb and the desserts linger long in the memory. The fixed price weekday lunch menu of a first and second course, wine and water is exceptional value. (☎06 4891 3832; Via del Boschetto 73; meals €45; ⏱closed Sun & Mon lunch; Ⓜ Cavour)

Agata e Romeo
MODERN ITALIAN €€€

10 ✖️ Map p82, E4

One of Rome's gastronomic pioneers, this fine-dining stalwart is still a presence in the city's culinary big league. Its forte is chef Agata Parisella's light, modern takes on classic Roman staples accompanied by superb wine from the restaurant's comprehensive and lovingly curated cellar. Bookings essential. (☎06 446 61 15; www.agatae romeo.it; Via Carlo Alberto 45; tasting menu €100-150; ⏱lunch & dinner Tue-Fri, dinner Mon & Sat; Ⓜ Vittorio Emanuele)

Panella L'Arte del Pane
CAFE, BAKERY €

11 ✖️ Map p82, E5

A devilishly tempting bakery-cum-cafe with a gluttonous array of *pizza al taglio* (pizza by the slice), focaccia, Sicilian rice balls, fried croquettes and pastries. You can sit outside – perfect for a leisurely breakfast or chilled evening drink – or perch on a high stool and eye up shelves of gastro delicacies as you munch. (Via Merulana 54; pizza slices from €2.50; ⏱8am-midnight Mon-Sat, 8.30am-4pm Sun; Ⓜ Vittorio Emanuele)

Palazzo del Freddo di Giovanni Fassi
GELATERIA €

12 ✖️ Map p82, H5

Sprinkled with old-fashioned marble tabletops and vintage gelato-making machinery, Rome's oldest ice-cream peddler is one of its best. Heavenly flavours include *riso* (rice), pistachio and *nocciola* (hazelnut), or you can opt for a delicious granita, served with a great dollop of cream. (Via Principe Eugenio 65-67; cones from €2; ⏱noon-10pm Tue-Thu, to midnight Fri & Sat, 10am-10pm Sun, longer hr summer; Ⓜ Vittorio Emanuele)

Doozo
JAPANESE €€

13 ✖️ Map p82, B3

Japanese nosh meets art and coffee-table tomes at this cool yet relaxed hybrid. Eye up contemporary photography exhibitions over a cup of roasted rice tea or relax in the Zen garden with tofu, sushi, *soba* (buckwheat noodle) soup and other Japanese delicacies. It's the perfect escape if you're craving a break from pasta. (☎06 481 56 55; www.doozo.it; Via Palermo 51; lunch

Local Life

Pasticceria Regoli

Italian tradition dictates that you take a tray of small cakes to mamma's for Sunday lunch. And **Pasticceria Regoli** (Map p82, E5; Via dello Statuto 60; ⊘6.45am-8.30pm Wed-Sun; Ⓜ Vittorio Emanuele) is where the locals come to buy their *dolci* (sweets). But you don't need an occasion to stop by. Just being in Rome is reason enough to treat yourself to one of its delicious creamy concoctions.

€15-25, dinner €35-45; ⊘lunch & dinner Tue-Sat, dinner Sun; ꤮Via Nazionale)

Mia Market   CAFE €

14 🍴 Map p82, B4

This is a good spot for a light lunch – an organic cafe and food shop with a few mismatched tables, crates of greenery and a daily selection of healthy homemade dishes. The onus is on seasonal, local ingredients so expect rustic quiches, couscous and cereals, legume salads, meatballs and biscuity desserts. (✆06 4782 4611; Via Panisperna 225; dishes from €5; ⊘10am-3.30pm & 5-10pm Mon-Sat; Ⓜ Cavour)

La Carbonara   TRATTORIA €€

15 🍴 Map p82, B4

A family-run trattoria on the go since 1906, this was a favourite hang-out of Enrico Fermi, one of the physicists behind the first atomic bomb. It's a lively place with brusque waiters, an energetic atmosphere and graffiti all over the walls – tradition dictates that diners should leave a message. The speciality of the house is the eponymous carbonara. (✆06 482 51 76; www.lacarbonara.it; Via Panisperna 214; meals €35-40; ⊘Mon-Sat; Ⓜ Cavour)

Da Ricci   PIZZERIA €

16 🍴 Map p82, B3

Tucked away on a cobbled cul-de-sac, Est! Est! Est! (as it's also known) is possibly Rome's oldest pizzeria. Beginning life as a wine shop in 1905, it's famed for its deep-crust *pizza alla napoletana* (Neapolitan-style pizza), served up in old-school surrounds packed with boisterous, satisfied regulars. (✆06 488 11 07; Via Genova 32; pizzas from €6; ⊘7pm-midnight Tue-Sun; ꤮Via Nazionale)

Drinking

Ai Tre Scalini   WINE BAR

17 🍷 Map p82, A4

Sporting the quintessential ivy-clad exterior, this vintage watering hole is always packed, with crowds spilling out of the tiny, pub-like interior onto the street. Apart from a tasty selection of wines it also serves a few choice beers and a heart-warming array of cheeses, olives and cold cuts. (Via Panisperna 251; ⊘12.30pm-1am Mon-Fri, 6pm-1am Sat & Sun; Ⓜ Cavour)

Bohemien BAR

18 Map p82, B4

Suitably offbeat with its worn velvet armchairs, modern art and silky tunes, this Left Bank–inspired bolthole is a picture. It draws a fittingly boho crowd who pack the place, looking good and drinking wine by the glass, after about 10.30pm. Come earlier, from 7pm, for the small-but-scrumptious *aperitivo* (aperitif) spread. (Via degli Zingari 36; ☺6pm-2am Wed-Mon; ⓂCavour)

Al Vino al Vino WINE BAR

19 Map p82, A4

Sporting a rustic-chic look – all terracotta floors, Sicilian-style ceramic-topped tables and contemporary paintings – this attractive *enoteca* (wine bar) is a Monti classic. It boasts a fine collection of wines, particularly *passiti* (sweet wines), a savvy selection of whiskies and grappas, and a small menu of snacks and Sicilian delicacies. (Via dei Serpenti 19; ⓂCavour)

La Bottega del Caffè CAFE

20 Map p82, A5

Contemporary, buzzing and situated right on picture-perfect Piazza Madonna dei Monti, this cafe is a real crowd-pleaser, ideal for whiling away any part of the day. Vino aside, you'll find fine coffee, freshly squeezed juices and grazing options ranging from simple pizzas to salads, cheeses and salamis. (Piazza Madonna dei Monti 5; ☺8am-2am; ⓂCavour)

Entertainment

Micca Club LIVE MUSIC, NIGHTCLUB

21 Map p82, H5

Rockabilly festivals, burlesque workshops, swing revival nights, DJ-spun dance sessions – this swinging basement club has most tastes catered for. Come pre-performance for *aperitivo* from 7pm to 10pm. There's an admission fee if a gig's on and at the weekend. Register online for discounts. (☎06 8744 0079; www.miccaclub.com; Via Pietra Micca 7a; ☺7pm-late Thu-Tue; ⓂVittorio Emanuele)

Charity Cafe LIVE MUSIC

22 Map p82, B4

Think narrow space, spindly tables, dim lighting and a laid-back vibe: this is the place to snuggle down and listen to some silky live jazz. Supremely civilised, relaxed and untouristy, it's very Monti. (www.charitycafe.it; Via Panisperna 68; ☺6pm-2am Tue-Sun; ⓂCavour)

Teatro dell'Opera di Roma OPERA HOUSE

23 Map p82, C2

Puccini premiered *Tosca* at Rome's opera house, whose stern fascist exterior belies a classic gilt-and-velvet interior. Performances are held throughout the season, alongside ballet and classical-music concerts. In July and August events move to the

Boutique fashion

spectacular Terme di Caracalla (p111). (📞06 48 16 01; www.operaroma.it; Piazza Beniamino Gigli 1; Ⓜ Repubblica)

Hangar
NIGHTCLUB

24 Map p82, C5

Rome's veteran gay bar is still a hit with local Lotharios and cruising out-of-towners, all of whom come for the down-to-earth yet raunchy vibe. For a kicking crowd, turn up on weekends, Mondays (porn night) or Thursdays (striptease). There's even a dark room for turned-on punters. (www.hangaronline.it; Via in Selci 69; 🕑 10.30pm-2.30am Wed-Mon; Ⓜ Cavour)

Shopping

Abito
FASHION

25 🔒 Map p82, A4

This is the studio-boutique of designer Wilma Silvestri, who reworks retro threads into chic, fashion-forward statements. Her *Confezione Express* range allows you to pick a style from 20 prototype garments and have it made in a colour and fabric of your choosing. She also hosts guest designers and sometimes holds vintage sales. (Via Panisperna 61; 🕑 10.30am-8pm Mon-Sat, noon-8pm Sun; Ⓜ Cavour)

La Bottega del Cioccolato
FOOD

26 🔒 Map p82, A5

Welcome to a magical world of scarlet walls and old-fashioned glass cabinets, of irresistible kitchen smells and lovingly homemade chocolates. Give in to wickedly smooth, freshly made pralines and truffles or warm your soul with thick hot chocolate (sold to take away at €3.50). (www.labottegadel cioccolato.it; Via Leonina 82; 🕑 9.30am-7.30pm Mon-Sat; Ⓜ Cavour)

Super
FASHION, ACCESSORIES

27 🔒 Map p82, B4

Lauded by French *Vogue* and Japanese *Elle*, minimalist, unisex Super ditches big-name bores for hard-to-find threads from up-and-coming European designers. There's also a quirky collection of designer novelties. (www.super-space.com; Via Leonina 42; ⊙10.30am-2pm Tue-Sat & 3.30-8pm Mon-Fri; Ⓜ Cavour)

Arion Esposizioni
BOOKSTORE, MUSIC STORE

The bookshop of the Palazzo delle Esposizioni (see 6 ◎ Map p82, A2), a stunning Firouz Galdo–designed space, is made for relaxed browsing with its white minimalist decor and themed collection of art, architecture and photography books and publications. You'll also find DVDs, CDs, vinyl, children's books and gadgets. (Via Milano 15/17; ⊙10am-8pm Mon-Thu & Sun, to 10.30pm Fri & Sat; ◻Via Nazionale)

Fausto Santini Outlet
SHOES

28 🔒 Map p82, C3

Close to the Basilica di Santa Maria Maggiore, this is the place to pick up end-of-line Fausto Santini boots, shoes and bags at a fraction of the retail price. Sizes are limited, however. (Via Cavour 106; Ⓜ Cavour)

Local Life
Shopping on Via del Boschetto

While Monti has no shortage of cool streets, **Via del Boschetto** (Map p82, A3) is the neighbourhood's stand-out strip. Its eclectic boutiques and bric-a-brac bolt-holes are perfect for picking up vintage clothes, costume jewellery and one-off fashions, all at affordable prices.

At No 148, **Fabio Piccioni** (⊙2-8pm Mon, 10.30am-1pm & 2-8pm Tue-Sat) is known for his deco-inspired jewellery that is lovingly crafted from old trinkets. Further up, at No 1d, Danish designer **Tina Sondergaard** (⊙10.30am-1pm & 1.30-7.30pm Tue-Sat, 3-7.30pm Mon) has made a name for herself with her limited-edition retro-esque ladies wear. At No 20, **Libreria La Gru** (⊙5-8pm Mon, 11am-2.30pm & 4-8pm Tue-Sat) is a lovely bookshop with rare books and first editions.

Local Life
San Lorenzo & Il Pigneto

Getting There

🚌 **Bus** Take bus 71 or 492 to San Lorenzo; buses 81, 810, 105 and n12 serve Pigneto.

🚊 **Tram** Take tram 3 for San Lorenzo, and tram 5, 14 or 19 for Pigneto.

A lively student quarter, San Lorenzo is a metropolitan mix of graffiti-clad streets, artists studios, cheap takeaways and hip restaurants. Apart from a major basilica, there are few traditional sights, but come evening the area bursts into life. Southeast, the former working-class Pigneto district is now one of the capital's coolest, a bar-heavy pocket frequented by bohemians, fun seekers and trend-setting urbanites.

1 Basilica di San Lorenzo Fuori-le-Mura

The starkly beautiful **Basilica di San Lorenzo Fuori-le-Mura** (Piazzale San Lorenzo; ⏱8am-noon & 4-7pm; 🚇Piazzale del Verano) sits on St Lawrence's burial place. Highlights include the Cosmati floor and the 13th-century frescoed portico. Next door, the **Cimitero di Campo Verano** (Piazzale del Verano; ⏱7.30am-6pm, to 5pm winter; 🚇Piazzale del Verano), Rome's largest cemetery, is a strangely moving place.

2 Chocolate at Said Antica Fabbrica del Cioccolato

For a change of scene, search out **Said Antica Fabbrica del Cioccolato** (www.said.it; Via Tiburtina 135; ⏱10am-12.30am Mon-Sat; 🚇Via Tiburtina). A delicious hideaway set in a 1920s factory, it's part shop – selling all sorts of exotic chocs – and part mod-creative restaurant (meals €50).

3 Modern Art at Pastificio Cerere

San Lorenzo's boho credentials express themselves to the full at the **Pastificio Cerere** (www.pastificiocerere.com; Via degli Ausoni 7; 🚇Via Tiburtina), a former pasta factory turned contemporary art collective. Home to artists studios, a gallery and courtyard space, it hosts regular exhibitions.

4 Dining at Pommidoro

Unchanged throughout San Lorenzo's metamorphosis from working-class district to bohemian enclave, century-old **Pommidoro** (📞06 445 26 92; Piazza dei Sanniti 44; meals €40; ⏱Mon-Sat; 🚇Via Tiburtina) is a much-loved local institution specialising in classic Roman pastas and delicious grilled meats.

5 Hang Out at Necci

Start your exploration of bar-studded Pigneto at iconic **Necci** (Via Fanfulla da Lodi 68; ⏱8am-1pm daily; 🚇Circonvallazione Casilina). The old stomping ground of cinema great Pier Paolo Pasolini, this laid-back cafe caters to an eclectic crowd of all ages, who come to down beers on the terrace or tuck into hearty grub to the sounds of Little Tony jukebox tunes.

6 Wine at Vini e Olii

Continue your bar-hopping with a glass of vino at **Vini e Olii** (Via del Pigneto 18; 🚇Circonvallazione Casilina), a traditional 'wine and oil' shop on Pigneto's main pedestrianised drag. It's all very spit-and-sawdust, with outdoor seating, cheap booze and tasty *porchetta* (herby, spit-roasted pork).

7 A Gig at Circolo degli Artisti

For the day's rousing finale catch a gig at the **Circolo degli Artisti** (www.circoloartisti.it; Via Casilina Vecchia 42; ⏱7pm-2am Tue-Thu, to 4.30am Fri-Sun; 🚇Via Casilina). East of Pigneto, this kicking club offers one of Rome's best nights out, with top live music from Italian and international bands, cracking DJ turns and a large garden area for outdoor beers. Admission is either free or a bargain.

Explore

Celio & Lateran

One of Rome's seven hills, the Celio (Caelian) rises to the south of
the Colosseum (Colosseo). It's a tranquil area of medieval churches
and graceful greenery, ideal for escaping the crowds but with little
after-hours action. At the top of the hill, the landmark Basilica di
San Giovanni in Laterano sits in splendour at the heart of the largely
residential San Giovanni district.

The Sights in a Day

Hop on the metro and head to San Giovanni. Exit the station, pass through Porta San Giovanni, and there, on your left, you'll see the monumental white facade of the **Basilica di San Giovanni in Laterano** (pictured left; p96). Once you've had your fill of mosaics and marble, stop off at **Via Sannio market** (p103) to look for a bargain, before doubling back down to the **Basilica di San Clemente** (p99) and its creepy underground corridors. Lunch on authentic Roman cuisine at **Il Bocconcino** (p101).

To walk off lunch head to **Villa Celimontana** (p100) to wait for the nearby **Chiesa di Santo Stefano Rotondo** (p99) to open for the afternoon. Study the church's grisly frescoes to see what fate lay in store for the early Christian martyrs, some of whom supposedly lived in the **Case Romane** (p99) under the Chiesa di SS Giovanni e Paolo.

Finish the day off with a wood-fired pizza at **Li Rioni** (p101) and jazz-fuelled drinks at **Il Pentagrappolo** (p103). Alternatively, feast on romantic Colosseum views and classy, contemporary cuisine at rooftop **Aroma** (p102).

 Top Sights

Basilica di San Giovanni in Laterano (p96)

Best of Rome

History
Basilica di San Clemente (p99)

Chiesa di SS Giovanni e Paolo & Case Romane (p99)

Basilica di San Giovanni in Laterano (p96)

Gay & Lesbian
Coming Out (p103)

Architecture
Basilica di San Giovanni in Laterano (p96)

Getting There

M Metro San Giovanni is accessible by metro line A. For the Celio, you can walk up from Colosseo or Circo Massimo stations (both line B).

🚌 Bus Useful bus routes include 85, 87 and 714, all of which stop near the Basilica di San Giovanni in Laterano.

Top Sights
Basilica di San Giovanni in Laterano

For a thousand years this monumental cathedral was the most important church in Christendom. Consecrated in AD 324, it was the first Christian basilica to be built in Rome and, until the 14th century, was the pope's main place of worship. It is now Rome's official cathedral and the pope's seat as Bishop of Rome. The oldest of Rome's four papal basilicas, it has twice been destroyed by fire and the church you see today is a culmination of several comprehensive makeovers.

👁 Map p98, D3

Piazza di San Giovanni in Laterano 4

basilica admission free, cloister €3

🕑 basilica 7am-6.30pm, cloister 9am-6pm

Ⓜ San Giovanni

Don't Miss

The Facade

Surmounted by 15 7m-high statues – Christ with St John the Baptist, John the Evangelist and the 12 Apostles – Alessandro Galilei's late-baroque facade dates to the mid-18th century. In the portico, the central **bronze doors** were moved here from the Curia in the Roman Forum, while to their right, the wooden **Holy Door** is only opened in Jubilee years.

The Nave

The echoing interior, largely the result of a mid-17th-century revamp by Borromini, is a breathtaking sight, measuring 130m (length) by 55.6m (width) by 30m (height). Beneath the spectacular gilt ceiling, the central nave is lined with 4.6m-high sculptures of the apostles, each set in a heroic pose in his own dramatic niche.

The Baldachin

At the head of the nave, a pointed Gothic baldachin (ceremonial canopy) rises over the papal altar. A dramatic work, set atop four columns and decorated with pictures of Jesus, the Virgin Mary and the saints, it houses the relics of St Peter's and St Paul's heads. In front, a double staircase leads to the **confessio** and the Renaissance tomb of Pope Martin V.

The Cloister

To the left of the altar, the beautiful 13th-century cloister is a lovely, peaceful place with graceful Cosmatesque (decorative stone inlay) twisted columns set around a **central garden**. Lining the ambulatories are marble fragments of the original basilica, including the remains of a 5th-century papal throne and inscriptions of a couple of papal bulls.

☑ Top Tips

▶ Audioguides are available for a voluntary donation from the desk in the central nave.

▶ Look down as well as up – the basilica has a beautiful 15th-century mosaic floor.

▶ It's worth paying the small fee to enter the peaceful cloister.

▶ Check out the Giotto fresco on the first column in the right-hand nave.

▶ For a virtual tour of the basilica, plus ecclesiastical soundtrack, check out www.vatican .va/various/basiliche/ san_giovanni/vr_tour/ index-it.html.

✕ Take a Break

There are few recommended eateries right by the basilica so you're better off finishing your tour and heading downhill towards the Colosseum. Here you can lunch on classic trattoria food at Il Bocconcino (p101) or grab a coffee at Coming Out (p103).

E Viale Manzoni

Via Nino Bixio

Via di Quintino

Via di Statilia

Via Emanuele Filiberto

Ⓜ Manzoni

Via Tasso

Via Tasso

Via Boiardo

Piazza di Porta San Giovanni

Ⓜ San Giovanni

Scala Santa & Sancta Sanctorum

Obelisk

Palazzo Lateran

Piazzale Appio

Basilica di San Giovanni in Laterano

Ⓜ 16

Via Amiterno

Via Santo

Via Lic

Via Magna Grecia

Via Velio

Via Veio

400 m
0.2 miles

D Via Galilei

Via Alfieri

Via Merulana

Via Merulana

Viale Manzoni

Piazza di San Giovanni in Laterano ◉ 6

Via di San Giovanni in Laterano

LATERAN

Battistero Lateranense

Via dell'Amba Aradam

Via Sant'Erasmo

Via Ferratella in Laterano

Via Ferratella in Laterano

Via Ipponio

For reviews see
◉ Top Sights	p96
◉ Sights	p99
✕ Eating	p101
◐ Drinking	p103
🛍 Shopping	p103

C Via Mecenate

Via Ruggero Bonghi

Via Murator

Via Crescimbeni

Piazza di San

Via Labicana

Via Guicciardini

Via P Villari

Via di San

Via Ⓜ 15

Basilica di San Clemente ◉ 1

Chiesa di San Clemente

Via di San Giovanni in Laterano ◉ 2

Santissimi Quattro Coronati 🛍 15

Chiesa di SS Quattro Coronati

Rotondo

Piazza Porta Metronia

Via Santo Stefano Rotondo

Piazzale Metronio

Via Gall

B Via del Normanni

Parco del Colle Oppio

Via della Domus Aurea

✕ 10

Via di SS Quattro Coronati

Via Capo d'Africa

✕ 8

Via M ✕ 13

Via Annia

Via Celimontana

Aurello

Chiesa di Via di Santo Stefano ◉ 3

Santo Stefano Rotondo

CELIO

A Ⓜ Colosseo

Via N Salvi

Parco del Colle Oppio

◉ 14

Via di SS Quattro Coronati ✕ 9

Via Ostilia

✕ 11

✕ 12

Via Celio Vibenna

Piazza del Colosseo

Viale del Parco del Celio

CAMPITELLI

Chiesa di SS Giovanni e Paolo & Case Romane ◉ 4

Clivo di Scauro

Piazza di SS Giovanni e Paolo ◉ 5

Villa Celimontana

Parco San Sebastiano

Via Claudia

Via della Croce

Via della Navicella

Via di Valle delle Camène

Viale delle Terme di Caracalla

Parco di Porta

1

2

3

4

Sights

Basilica di San Clemente
CHURCH

1 Map p98, B2

This is a case of architectural time travel: a 12th-century basilica plonked on a 4th-century church, which, in turn, stands over a 2nd-century pagan temple and 1st-century Roman house. Beneath everything a subterranean river runs through a Roman Republic–era drain. Highlights include the main basilica's 12th-century apse mosaic and the eerie underground temple to the Persian god Mithras. (www.basilicasanclemente.com; Via di San Giovanni in Laterano; church/excavations free/€5; ⏱9am-12.30pm & 3-6pm Mon-Sat, noon-6pm Sun; Ⓜ Colosseo)

Chiesa di SS Quattro Coronati
CHURCH

2 Map p98, C2

This brooding 4th-century church, which was rebuilt as a fortified convent after being destroyed by Normans in 1084, sports a 9th-century bell tower and apse, and a soothing 13th-century cloister. The pièces de résistance, however, are the exquisite 13th-century frescoes depicting St Sylvester and Constantine in the Cappella di San Silvestro. Ring the bell for a peek. (Via dei Santissimi Quattro Coronati 20; ⏱church 6.15am-8pm Mon-Sat, 6.45am-12.30pm & 3-7.30pm Sun, Cappella di San Silvestro & cloisters 9.30am-noon & 4.30-6pm Mon-Sat, 9-10.40am & 4-5.45pm Sun; 🚃Via Labicana)

Chiesa di Santo Stefano Rotondo
CHURCH

3 Map p98, B3

Built in the 5th century, Rome's first round church features graphic 16th-century frescoes – currently being cleaned up – depicting the tortures suffered by Christian martyrs. All the boiling and hacking was too much for Charles Dickens, who remarked: 'Such a panorama of horror and butchery no man could imagine in his sleep, though he were to eat a whole pig, raw, for supper'. (www.santo-stefano-rotondo.it; Via di Santo Stefano Rotondo 7; ⏱9.30am-12.30pm & 2-5pm Tue-Sat winter, 9.30am-12.30pm & 3-6pm Tue-Sun summer; 🚃Via della Navicella)

Chiesa di SS Giovanni e Paolo & Case Romane
HISTORICAL SITE

4 Map p98, A3

Beneath the uninspiring 4th-century church lie the engrossing **Case Romane** (📞06 7045 4544; www.caseromane.it; adult/reduced €6/4; ⏱10am-1pm & 3-6pm Thu-Mon), a frescoed maze of ancient abodes where apostles John and Paul supposedly lived for a while. There's no direct evidence for this, although research has revealed that the houses were used for Christian worship. Entry is to the side of the church. (Piazza di SS Giovanni e Paolo; ⏱8.30am-noon & 3.30-6pm Mon-Thu; Ⓜ Colosseo or Circo Massimo)

Villa Celimontana
PARK

5 Map p98, A3

With its lawns and colourful flower beds, this tranquil hilltop park is a wonderful place to escape the crowds and revel in the quiet amid lush pine trees and a sprinkling of Roman ruins. At its centre is a 16th-century villa that was once owned by the Mattei family but now houses the Italian Geographical Society. (☉7am-sunset; 🚌Via della Navicella)

Battistero Lateranense
CHURCH

6 Map p98, D3

On Piazza di San Giovanni in Laterano, itself dominated by Rome's oldest and tallest **obelisk**, is this fascinating octagonal baptistery. Built by Constantine in the 4th century, it served as the prototype for later Christian churches and bell towers. The chief interest, apart from the architecture, are the decorative mosaics, some of which date back to the 5th century. (Piazza di San Giovanni in Laterano; ☉7am-12.30pm & 4-7pm; Ⓜ San Giovanni)

Scala Santa & Sancta Sanctorum
CHURCH

7 Map p98, E2

The Scala Santa is said to be the staircase that Jesus walked up in Pontius Pilate's palace in Jerusalem. The 28 steps are so holy that pilgrims climb them on their knees. At the top, and

Understand
Donation of Constantine

- - - - - - - - - - - - - - - - -

The frescoes in the Chiesa di SS Quattro Coronati tell the story of the Donation of Constantine, the most famous forgery in medieval history. The Donation was a document in which the Roman Emperor Constantine purportedly granted Pope Sylvester I (r AD 314–35) and his successors control of Rome and the Western Roman Empire, as well as primacy over the holy sees of Antioch, Alexandria, Constantinople, Jerusalem and all of the world's churches. The alleged reason for Constantine's generosity was the gratitude he felt to Sylvester for his curing him of leprosy.

No one is exactly sure when the document was written but the consensus is that it dates to the mid- or late-8th century. Certainly this fits with the widespread theory that the author was a Roman cleric, possibly working with the knowledge of Pope Stephen II (r 752–57).

For centuries the Donation was used by popes to justify their territorial claims against the Holy Roman emperors and other rival leaders. But in 1440 the Italian humanist and philosopher Lorenzo Valla proved that it was a forgery. By analysing the Latin used in the document he was able to show that it was inconsistent with the Latin used in the 4th century.

Scala Santa

accessible by two side staircases, is the richly frescoed **Sancta Sanctorum** (Holy of Holies), once the pope's private chapel. (Piazza di San Giovanni in Laterano 14; Scala Santa/Sancta Sanctorum free/€3.50; ⏰Scala Santa 6.15am-noon & 3.30-6.30pm summer, 6.15am-noon & 3-6pm winter, Sancta Sanctorum 9.30am-noon & 3-5pm, closed Wed am & Sun year-round; MSan Giovanni)

Eating

Li Rioni   PIZZERIA €

8 ✕ Map p98, B2

Locals swear by Li Rioni, arriving for the second seating around 9pm once the tourists have left. A classic neighbourhood pizzeria, it buzzes

most nights as diners squeeze into the cosy interior – cheerfully set up as a Roman street scene – and tuck into excellent wood-fired pizzas and crispy *supplì* (fried rice balls). (✆06 7045 0605; Via dei Santissimi Quattro Coronati 24; pizzas from €6; ⏰dinner Wed-Mon; MColosseo)

Il Bocconcino   TRATTORIA €€

9 ✕ Map p98, B2

An old-school Roman trattoria good for lunch after a morning at the Colosseum. With its gingham tablecloths, outdoor seating and cosy interior, it looks like all the other eateries in this touristy neighbourhood but it stands out for its spot-on pastas and imaginative main courses. (✆06 7707 9175;

Understand
Mithraism

Mithraism was a cult that was hugely popular with the ancient Roman military. According to its mythology, Mithras, a young, handsome god, was ordered to slay a wild bull by the Sun. As the bull died, it gave life, as its blood flow caused wheat and other plants to grow. In Mithraic iconography, a serpent and dog are usually shown attacking the bull to try to prevent this, while a scorpion attacks its testicles.

Devotees underwent complex processes of initiation, and ate bread and water as a representation of the body and the blood of the bull. Sound familiar? The early Christians thought so too, and were fervently against the cult, feeling its practices were too close to their own.

www.ilbocconcino.com; Via Ostilia 23; meals €30-35; ⊙Thu-Tue, closed Aug; MColosseo)

Aroma
GASTRONOMIC €€€

10 Map p98, B1

If you're one for a romantic dinner, the rooftop restaurant of the five-star Palazzo Manfredi hotel offers unforgettable 'marry me' views of the Colosseum and food that rises to the occasion. Overseeing the kitchen is chef Giuseppe Di Iorio, whose brand of forward-looking Italian cuisine has won widespread applause from critics and diners alike. (☑06 9761 5109; www.palazzomanfredi.com; Palazzo Manfredi, Via Labicana 125; meals €100, tasting menu €125; MColosseo)

Taverna dei Quaranta
TRADITIONAL ITALIAN €€

11 Map p98, B2

Tasty traditional food, honest prices, near the Colosseum but off the beaten track – there's a lot to like about this laid-back, airy trattoria. There are no great surprises on the menu, but daily specials add variety and all the desserts are homemade – always a good sign. (☑06 700 05 50; www.tavernadeiquaranta.com; Via Claudia 24; pizzas from €7, meals €25-30; ⊙Mon-Sat; MColosseo)

Crab
SEAFOOD €€€

12 Map p98, A2

Located in a converted warehouse, just steps from the Colosseum, upmarket Crab serves obscenely good seafood presented with a distinctly Sardinian slant. Standout choices include the *crudi* (raw fish), especially the oysters, and the luxurious *aragosta alla catalana* (Catalonian lobster). (☑06 7720 3636; Via Capo d'Africa 2; meals €70-80; ⊙lunch & dinner Tue-Sat, dinner Mon; MColosseo)

Drinking

Il Pentagrappolo WINE BAR

13 Map p98, B2

Star-vaulted Il Pentagrappolo is the ideal antidote to sightseeing overload. Join its mellow, laid-back crowd to sip on wine and chat over piano tunes or relax to live jazz on Thursday, Friday and Saturday evenings. There's also lunch and daily *aperitivi* (aperitifs) from 6pm. (www.ilpentagrappolo.com; Via Celimontana 21b; ⊘noon-3pm & 6pm-1am Tue-Fri, 6pm-1am Sat & Sun; Ⓜ Colosseo)

Coming Out BAR

14 Map p98, B1

On warm evenings, with lively crowds on the street and the Colosseum as a backdrop, there are few sweeter places to knock back a beer than this intimate, DJ-spun bar. Predominantly queer, it's a popular pre-clubbing stop and a handy spot for a cheap, simple bite, too. (www.comingout.it; Via di San Giovanni in Laterano 8; ⊘10.30am-2am; Ⓜ Colosseo)

Shopping

Soul Food MUSIC STORE

15 Map p98, C2

Run by **Hate Records** (www.haterecords .com), Soul Food feeds music hunters on a diet of rare vintage vinyl. Flip through the racks and score anything from Hendrix and the Stooges to electro and low-fi punk. Retro-design T-shirts and offbeat novelties keep pop-trash aficionados grinning. (Via di San Giovanni in Laterano 192; ⊘10.30am-1.30pm & 3.30-8pm Tue-Sat; Ⓜ San Giovanni)

Via Sannio MARKET

16 Map p98, E4

Update your wardrobe staples at this buzzing morning market. Expect piles of new and vintage clothing, cheap denim, leather jackets and bargain-priced shoes – patient rummagers are amply rewarded. (⊘8am-1pm Mon-Sat; Ⓜ San Giovanni)

Top Sights
Appian Way

Getting There

The Appian Way runs southeast from Porta San Sebastiano, south of the Celio.

🚌 **Bus** Take bus 660 from Colli Albani metro (line A) or bus 118 from Piramide (line B).

Completed in 190 BC, ancient Rome's *regina viarum* (queen of roads) connected the capital with Brindisi on Italy's southern Adriatic coast. Nowadays, the Appian Way (Via Appia Antica) is one of Rome's most exclusive addresses, a beautiful cobbled thoroughfare flanked by grassy fields, ancient ruins and towering pine trees. But it has a dark history – it was here that Spartacus and 6000 of his slave rebels were crucified, and the early Christians buried their dead in the underground catacombs.

Don't Miss

Mausoleo di Cecilia Metella

Dating to the 1st century BC, the drum-like
Mausoleo di Cecilia Metella (Via Appia Antica 161;
admission incl Terme di Caracalla & Villa dei Quintili adult/
reduced €7/4; ⏰9am-1hr before sunset) was built as
a burial chamber for the daughter of the consul
Quintus Metellus Creticus. In the 14th century
it was fortified by the Caetani family, who would
bully passing traffic into paying a toll.

Villa di Massenzio

The highlight of the **Villa di Massenzio** (www.villa
dimassenzio.it; Via Appia Antica 153; adult/reduced €5/4;
⏰9am-4pm Tue-Sat), Maxentius' 4th-century imperial palace, is the Circo di Massenzio, Rome's
best-preserved chariot racetrack – you can still
make out the starting stalls of the 10,000-seat
arena. The palace's unexcavated ruins sit above
the racetrack's northern end. Nearby, Maxentius
built the imposing Tomb of Romulus for his son.

Basilica e Catacombe di San Sebastiano

Birthplace of the term 'catacomb' (the underground burial site was located 'near a quarry',
kata kymbas in Greek), the **Catacombe di San
Sebastiano** (www.catacombe.org; Via Appia Antica
136; adult/reduced €8/5; ⏰10am-5pm Mon-Sat, closed
mid-Nov–mid-Dec) boasts three perfectly preserved
mausoleums with original 2nd-century frescoes,
mosaics and stucco. Above ground, the much-
tweaked 4th-century basilica stands on the site
where St Sebastian was martyred and buried in
the late 3rd century.

Catacombe di San Callisto

The largest and busiest of Rome's catacombs, the
2nd-century **Catacombe di San Callisto** (www.cata
combe.roma.it; Via Appia Antica 110 & 126; adult/reduced €8/5;

📞06 513 53 16

www.parcoappia
antica.it

🖼Via Appia Antica

☑ Top Tips

▶ Visit on Sundays to
avoid traffic. On other
days the stretch from
Porta San Sebastiano
isn't pedestrian friendly.

▶ Get info on tours and
bike hire from the **Appia
Antica Regional Park
Information Point** (www
.parcoappiaantica.it; Via
Appia Antica 58-60)

▶ If you're short on time,
hit Villa di Massenzio
and nearby Basilica
e Catacombe di San
Sebastiano.

▶ After your visit, head
to Testaccio (p112) for
a taste of authentic
Roman cooking.

✗ Take a Break

Head to **L'Archeologia**
(📞06 788 04 94; www
.larcheologia.it; Via Appia
Antica 139; meals about
€50 ⏰closed Tue; 🖼Via
Appia Antica) for au-
thentic regional fare
served in a former
staging post.

⏱9am-noon & 2-5pm Thu-Tue, closed mid-Jan–mid-Feb) served as the first official cemetery of the Roman Catholic Church. St Cecilia was buried here, and in the 20km of tunnels explored to date, archaeologists have found the tombs of 500,000 people and seven martyred popes.

Understand
The Catacombs

Built as communal burial grounds, the catacombs were the early Christians' solution to the problem of what to do with their dead. Belief in the Resurrection meant that they couldn't cremate their corpses, as was the custom at the time, and ancient Roman law forbade burial within the city walls. Furthermore, as a persecuted minority they didn't have their own cemeteries. So, in the 2nd century they began to dig beneath Via Appia Antica, where a number of converted Christians already had family tombs.

Over time, as Christianity became more popular, competition for burial space became fierce and a cut-throat trade in tomb real estate developed. However, by the late 4th century, Christianity had been legalised and the Christians began to bury their dead near the basilicas within the city walls. By the Middle Ages the catacombs had been all but abandoned.

Catacombe di Santa Domitilla

Among Rome's oldest, the **Catacombe di Santa Domitilla** (www.domitilla.info; Via delle Sette Chiese 283; adult/reduced €8/5; ⏱9am-noon & 2-5pm Wed-Mon, closed Jan) were established on the private burial ground of Flavia Domitilla, niece of Emperor Domitian. Among the pagan and Christian wall paintings are around 2000 unopened tombs and the subterranean 4th-century **Chiesa di SS Nereus e Achilleus**, dedicated to two martyred Roman soldiers.

Chiesa del Domine Quo Vadis?

The pint-sized **Chiesa del Domine Quo Vadis?** (Via Appia Antica 51; ⏱8am-6.30pm Mon-Fri, 8.15am-6.45pm Sat & Sun winter, to 7.30pm Mon-Fri & 7.45pm Sat & Sun summer) marks the spot where St Peter met a vision of Jesus. When Peter asked: 'Domine, quo vadis?' ('Lord, where are you going?'), Jesus replied 'Venio Roman iterum crucifigi' ('I am coming to Rome to be crucified again'). Reluctantly, Peter joined him and tramped back into town to be arrested and executed.

Porta San Sebastiano

Marking the start of Via Appia Antica, the 5th-century **Porta San Sebastiano** (www.museodellemuraroma.it; Via di Porta San Sebastiano 18; adult/reduced €5/4; ⏱9am-2pm Tue-Sun) is the largest and best preserved of the gates in the **Aurelian Wall**. Inside, the modest Museo delle Mure illustrates the wall's history and gives the chance to walk along the top of the wall.

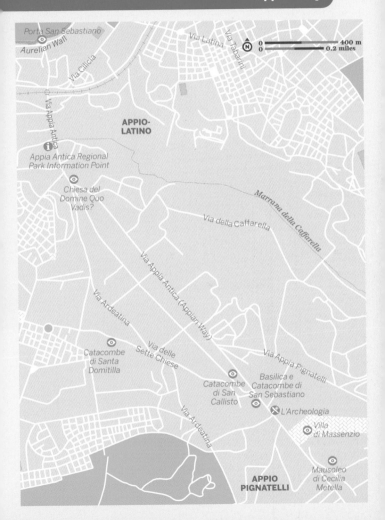

Explore

Aventino & Testaccio

Rising above the mighty ruins of the Terme di Caracalla, the Aventino (Aventine hill) is a graceful district of Liberty villas, lush gardens and austere churches. At the top, romantic Via di Santa Sabina boasts one of Rome's great curiosities – a keyhole view of St Peter's dome. Below, the traditional working-class district of Testaccio is a popular nightlife hang-out and a bastion of classical Roman cuisine.

The Sights in a Day

☀ Start your day with an imaginary workout at the **Terme di Caracalla** (pictured left; p111), one of ancient Rome's largest leisure centres. Once you're done, push on to Testaccio for a taste of neighbourhood life. Join the locals for a nose around the **Nuovo Mercato di Testaccio** (p117), stop for a coffee at **Linari** (p115) and then grab a bite from top takeaway **00100 Pizza** (p113).

☀ See in the afternoon at the **Cimitero Acattolico per gli Stranieri** (p112), the final resting place of Romantic heroes Shelley and Keats, before hiking up to the Aventino. It's quite a walk but worth it for the remarkable keyhole view from **Piazza dei Cavalieri di Malta** (p111) and the heart-melting panoramas from **Parco Savello** (p111). While you're up here make sure to look in to the gloriously austere **Basilica di Santa Sabina** (p111).

☾ Spend the evening in Testaccio, testing the neighbourhood's reputation as a culinary and nightlife hot spot. Dine on fab Italian fare at **Flavio al Velavevodetto** (p112) and then let your hair down at clubbing favourite **Conte Staccio** (p115).

 Best of Rome

Eating
Flavio al Velavevodetto (p112)

00100 Pizza (p113)

Il Gelato (p114)

Architecture
Terme di Caracalla (p111)

Basilica di Santa Sabina (p111)

Nightlife
Conte Staccio (p115)

Shopping
Volpetti (p116)

Nuovo Mercato di Testaccio (p117)

Culture
Terme di Caracalla (p111)

Villaggio Globale (p116)

Conte Staccio (p115)

Gay & Lesbian
L'Alibi (p116)

Getting There

Ⓜ **Metro** For Testacio take line B to Piramide. The Aventino is walkable from Testaccio and Circo Massimo (line B), although it's a bit of a hike from Circo Massimo.

🚌 **Bus** Take bus 714 to the Terme di Caracalla and bus 175 to the Aventino.

CAMPITELLI

Parco San Sebastiano

Via di San Gregorio

Via di Valle delle Camene

Viale delle Terme di Caracalla

Terme di Caracalla

1

Parco di Porta Capena

Piazza di Santa Balbina

Via Antonina

Viale Guido Baccelli

Via Guido

Viale di Villa Pepoli

Via del Cerchi

Circo Massimo

UN Food & Agriculture Organisation (FAO)

Via Aventino

Viale Aventino

Via del Circo Massimo

Via Terme Deciane

Via di Fonte di Fauno

Roseto Comunale

Clivo de Publici

Via di Prisca

Piazza Santa Prisca

Via Aventina

12

Via Bramante

Via A Palladio

Via C Maratta

Viale Giotto

Viale di Porta Ardeatina

Viale Marco Po

For reviews see

⊙ Sights	p111
⊗ Eating	p112
⊗ Drinking	p115
⊙⊙ Entertainment	p115
⊙ Shopping	p116

0 ———— 200 m

Parco Savello

4

Basilica di Santa Sabina

2

Via di Santa Sabina

Piazza dei Cavalieri di Malta

3

Via di San Alessio

Via Melania

Viale M Gelsomini

Piazza Albania

Piazza della Piramide Cestia

Via Flaminio Ponzio

Piramide di Caio Cestio

Piramide

M

Piazzale Ostiense

Stazione Roma-Ostia

Porta di Ripa Grande

Lgt Aventino

Porta Portuense

Via di San Michele

Via Amica

Piazzale Portuense Sublicio

Ponte Portuense Sublicio

Lgt Testaccio

Via Marmorata

15

16

14

Via G G Belli

Via B Franca

Via Manuzzi

17

Piazza Testaccio

Via Mastro Giorgio

Santa Maria Liberatrice

9

Via Florio

22

24

10

11

Via Luca della Robbia

Via Ginori

Via Nicola Zabaglia

Via Volta

Via Manuzio Zabaglia

23

13

Via Galvani

Cimitero Acattolico per gli Stranieri

5

Via Caio Cestio

Via di Monte Testaccio

Monte Testaccio

8

20

MACRO Testaccio

7

Piazza Orazio Giustiniani

Via Beniamino Franklin

19

Lgt Portuense

Tiber River

Sights

Terme di Caracalla ANCIENT RUINS

1 Map p110, E2

The hulking remains of Caracalla's baths' complex are among Rome's most awe-inspiring ruins. In the 3rd century, between 6000 and 8000 people visited the 10-hectare complex daily, while beneath the baths, gymnasiums, libraries, shops and gardens, hundreds of slaves tended to the plumbing systems in 9.5km of tunnels. Most of what you see today are the ruins of the central bath house. (Viale delle Terme di Caracalla 52; adult/reduced incl Mausoleo di Cecilia Metella & Villa dei Quintili €7/4; 9am-2pm Mon, 9am-1hr before sunset Tue-Sun; Via delle Terme di Caracalla)

Basilica di Santa Sabina CHURCH

2 Map p110, C1

This haunting 5th-century basilica boasts one of the oldest Crucifixion scenes in existence – in the top left of the cypress-wood doors, it depicts Jesus and the two thieves, although, strangely, not their crosses. Inside, the three austere naves are separated by 24 custom-made Corinthian columns, and Muñoz de Zamora, one of the Dominican's founding fathers, is buried here. (Piazza Pietro d'Illiria 1; 8.15am-12.30pm & 3.30-6pm; Lungotevere Aventino)

Piazza dei Cavalieri di Malta PIAZZA

3 Map p110, B1

Named after the Knights of Malta, who have their Roman headquarters here, in the **Priorato dei Cavalieri di Malta**, this ornate cypress-shaded square is famous for its secret view. Look through the keyhole in the Priorato's main door and you'll see the dome of St Peter's perfectly aligned at the end of a hedge-lined avenue. (Lungotevere Aventino)

Parco Savello PARK

4 Map p110, C1

Painters, love-struck teens and unfazed felines adore this pocket-sized park dubbed the *Giardino degli Aranci* (Orange Garden) for its sprinkling of lush, scented orange trees. Sit

Top Tip

Terme di Caracalla Extras

If you like opera, check www.operaroma.it for details of summer performances at the Terme di Caracalla. Also, if you visit the Terme, note that your ticket includes access to two other sites: the Mausoleo di Cecilia Metella and the Villa dei Quintili. However, both of these are some distance from the Terme – the Mausoleo on Via Appia Antica and Villa dei Quintili on Via Appia Nuova – and require a bus journey to get there.

Basilica di Santa Sabina (p111)

back on the terrace and watch the sun sink over the city to the sounds of church bells, wind and sirens. (Via di Santa Sabina; ⏱7am-6pm Oct-Feb, to 8pm Mar & Sep, to 9pm Apr-Aug; 🚊Lungotevere Aventino)

Cimitero Acattolico per gli Stranieri
CEMETERY

5 ◉ Map p110, B4

Despite the roads that surround it, Rome's Protestant Cemetery is a surprisingly tranquil place. Percy Bysshe Shelley wrote: 'It might make one in love with death to think that one should be buried in so sweet a place'. And so he was, along with fellow poet John Keats and a whole host of luminaries, including Antonio Gramsci,

founder of Italy's Communist Party. (Via Caio Cestio 5; voluntary donation €3; ⏱9am-5pm Mon-Sat, to 1pm Sun; Ⓜ Piramide)

Piramide di Caio Cestio
LANDMARK

6 ◉ Map p110, C4

Sticking out like, well, an Egyptian pyramid, this distinctive landmark stands in the Aurelian Wall at the side of a busy traffic junction. A 36m-high marble-and-brick tomb, it was built for Gaius Cestius, a 1st-century-BC magistrate, and some 200 years later was incorporated into the Aurelian fortification near Porta San Paolo. (Ⓜ Piramide)

MACRO Testaccio
GALLERY

7 ◉ Map p110, A4

Housed in Rome's ex-slaughterhouse, MACRO's second gallery serves up experimental art in two cavernous industrial halls. Note that it only opens when there's an exhibition on – check the website for details. (www.macro .roma.museum; Piazza Orazio Giustiniani 4; adult/reduced €5/3; ⏱4-10pm Tue-Sun; 🚊Via Marmorata)

Eating

Flavio al Velavevodetto
TRADITIONAL ITALIAN €€

8 ✖ Map p110, B3

This welcoming Testaccio eatery is the sort of place that gives Roman

Local Life
Monte Testaccio

Get to the heart of the local landscape at **Monte Testaccio** (Map p110, A4; 06 06 08; Via Nicolo Zabaglia 24 cnr Via Galvani; group visits by guided tour only, adult/reduced €4/3 plus cost of tour bus; 🚇Via Marmorata), a 45m-high artificial hill. In ancient times, when Testaccio was a river port, empty terracotta amphorae were discarded in the Tiber. But when the river became unnavigable, the pots were smashed and the pieces stacked in a pile, which over time grew into Monte Testaccio. Visit by appointment.

trattorias a good name. Housed in a rustic Pompeian-red villa, complete with intimate covered courtyard and an open-air terrace, it specialises in earthy, no-nonsense Italian food, prepared with skill and served in mountainous portions. Expect homemade pastas seasoned with fresh vegies and local *guanciale* (cured pig's cheek), and uncomplicated meaty mains. (📞06 574 41 94; www.flavioalvelavevodetto.it; Via di Monte Testaccio 97-99; meals €35; ⏱closed Sat lunch & Sun summer; 🚇Via Marmorata)

00100 Pizza   PIZZA AL TAGLIO €

9   Map p110, A3

A pocket-size pizza pusher, this is one of a select group of Roman takeaways with culinary ambitions. As well as pizzas topped with unusual combos –

imagine cream of chickpea or mozzarella, gorgonzola and port – you can snack on excellent *supplì* (crunchy rice croquettes) and *trapizzini*. These copyrighted creations are small cones of pizza stuffed with fillers such as *polpette al sugo* (meatballs in tomato sauce). (Via Giovanni Branca 88; pizza slices from €3; ⏱noon-11pm; 🚇Via Marmorata)

Da Felice   TRADITIONAL ITALIAN €€

10   Map p110, B3

A hit with locals, foodies and film director Roberto Benigni, who once wrote an ode to the place, Da Felice is a Testaccio institution. The decor might be post-industrial chic – exposed-brick walls, chequered marble floor, hanging lamps – but the menu remains true to its Roman roots, whether it's buttery offal or a soothing *saltimbocca* (veal cutlet with ham and sage). Book ahead. (📞06 574 68 00; www.felicetestaccio.com; Via Mastro Giorgio 29; meals €35-40; 🚇Via Marmorata)

Volpetti Più   TRADITIONAL ITALIAN €

11   Map p110, B3

One of the few places in Rome where you can sit down and stuff yourself silly for less than €20, Volpetti Più is a sumptuous *tavola calda* (buffet), offering a wide choice of pizzas, pastas, soups, meats, vegetables and golden-fried nibbles. Arrive early or be prepared to queue. (Via Alessandro Volta 8; mains €8 ⏱10.30am-3.30pm & 5.30-9.30pm Mon-Sat; 🚇Via Marmorata)

Understand
Roman Cuisine

Like many Italian regional cuisines, classic Roman cooking was born out of poverty and the judicious use of seasonal, local ingredients.

Offal
One of the trademarks of true Roman cuisine is offal, the so-called *quinto quarto* (fifth quarter). This taste for nose-to-tail eating arose in Testaccio around the city abattoir. Butchers working there used to be given offcuts to supplement their wages and, in order to make them edible, developed new recipes and cooking techniques. The resulting dishes proved popular, and still today *pajata* (veal intestines), *trippa* (tripe) and *coda alla vaccinara* (oxtail stew) are prized city staples.

Roman-Jewish Food
Much Roman cuisine is Jewish in origin, based on dishes that the city's Jewish community developed during centuries of confinement in the ghetto. Two dishes stand out: *carciofi alla giudia* (deep-fried artichoke) and *fiori di zucca fritti* (fried courgette flowers stuffed with mozzarella and anchovies).

Signature Dishes
Other iconic Roman dishes include *spaghetti alla carbonara* (with egg, cheese and *guanciale* bacon), *bucatini all'amatriciana* (thick spaghetti with tomato sauce and *guanciale*), *cacio e pepe* (pasta with salty *pecorino* cheese and pepper) and *saltimbocca* (veal cutlet with ham and sage).

Il Gelato
GELATERIA €

12 Map p110, D2

Claudio Torcè is one of Rome's gelato deities and his creamy revelations are seasonal, preservative-free and creative – expect flavours from ginger to gorgonzola. The zabaglione *semifreddo* is especially good and best devoured in a waffle *conchiglia* (shell), drizzled with your choice of home-made *caramello* (syrup). (Viale Aventino 59; ⏱11am-9pm Tue-Sun, to 10.30pm daily summer; Ⓜ Circo Massimo)

Checchino dal 1887
TRADITIONAL ITALIAN €€€

13 Map p110, A4

A pig's whisker from the city's former slaughterhouse, this is one of the grander restaurants specialising in the *quinto quarto* (fifth quarter – or insides of the animal). House speci-alities include *coda alla vaccinara* (oxtail stew) and *rigatoni alla gricia* (pasta tubes with *pecorino* cheese, black pepper and pancetta). (☑06 574 63 18; www.checchino-dal-1887.com; Via di

Monte Testaccio 30; meals €60; ⊗Tue-Sat, closed Aug; 🚇Via Marmorata)

Pizzeria Remo
PIZZERIA €

14 Map p110, A2

Though not a place for a romantic tête-à-tête, Remo is one of Rome's best-loved pizzerias, its spartan interior always crowded with noisy diners. Tick your choices on a sheet of paper slapped down by an overstretched waiter and wait for your huge, sizzling, charred-base disc. Expect to queue after 8.30pm. (☏06 574 62 70; Piazza Santa Maria Liberatrice 44; pizzas from €5.50; ⊗7pm-1am Mon-Sat; 🚇Via Marmorata)

Trattoria da Bucatino
TRADITIONAL ITALIAN €€

15 Map p110, B2

This laid-back neighbourhood trattoria is hugely popular. Ask for a table upstairs (with wood panels, chianti bottles and a mounted boar's head) and dig into huge portions of *bucatini all'amatriciana* and other typical Roman dishes. (☏06 574 68 86; Via Luca della Robbia 84; meals €30; ⊗Tue-Sun; 🚇Via Marmorata)

Drinking

L'Oasi della Birra
BAR

16 Map p110, B3

Under the Palombi *enoteca* (wine bar), this popular cellar bar is exactly what it says it is – an Oasis of Beer.

With everything from Teutonic heavyweights to boutique brews, as well as an ample wine list, aperitif buffet (5pm to 8.30pm) and menu of cheeses, cold cuts, stews and the like, it's ideal for an evening's carousing. (☏06 574 61 22; Piazza Testaccio 41; ⊗5pm-1am Mon-Thu & Sun, to 2am Fri & Sat; 🚇Via Marmorata)

Linari
CAFE

17 Map p110, A3

An authentic neighbourhood hangout, Linari remains local down to its plastic pavement chairs and gossiping mothers. It has the busy clatter of a good bar, with excellent pastries, splendid coffee and plenty of barside banter. There are a few outside tables which, if you can get one, are ideal for a cheap lunch (pastas/main courses €5.50/6.50). (Via Nicola Zabaglia 9; ⊗7am-11pm Wed-Mon; 🚇Via Marmorata)

Entertainment

Conte Staccio
NIGHTCLUB

18 Map p110, B4

With an under-the-stars terrace and cool, arched interior, Conte Staccio is one of the most popular venues on the Testaccio clubbing strip. Daily gigs by emerging groups set the tone, spanning indie pop, rock, acoustic, funk and electronic. Admission is usually free during the week. (www.contestaccio.com; Via di Monte Testaccio 65b; ⊗7pm-5am Tue-Sun; 🚇Via Marmorata)

Top Tip

Clubbing Notes

Clubs tend to get busy after midnight, or even after 2am. Often admission is free, but drinks are expensive, with cocktails typically costing from €10 to €16. Note also that it pays to dress up if you want to get in and fit in.

Villaggio Globale

NIGHTCLUB, LIVE MUSIC

19 Map p110, A4

For a warehouse-party vibe, head to Rome's best-known *centro sociale* (an ex-squat turned cultural centre) in the city's graffiti-sprayed former slaughterhouse. Loaded with dreadlocks, cheap beer and left-wing, antiracist consciousness, it delivers live gigs and DJ sessions, mostly dancehall, reggae, dubstep and drum 'n' bass. (www.ecn .org/villaggioglobale/joomla; Via Monte dei Cocci 22; ⊠Via Marmorata)

L'Alibi

NIGHTCLUB

20 Map p110, A4

One of Rome's best-known gay clubs, L'Alibi does high-camp with style, putting on kitsch shows and playing sultry, soulful house to a mixed gay and straight crowd. It's spread over three floors and if the sweaty atmosphere in the dance halls gets too much, head up to the summer roof terrace. Thursday nights are big, with the ever-popular Gloss party. (www .lalibi.it; Via di Monte Testaccio 44; ⊙11.30pm-5am Thu-Sun; ⊠Via Marmorata)

Akab Roma

NIGHTCLUB

21 Map p110, B4

This eclectic former workshop has an underground cellar, upper floor, garden and whimsical door policy. It gets rammed with twenty-somethings at weekends and serves up a steady stream of commercial house and mainstream tunes. Entrance is usually around €15, including a complimentary drink. (Via di Monte Testaccio 68-9; ⊙11pm-4am Tue-Sat, closed late Jun–mid-Sep; ⊠Via Marmorata)

Shopping

Volpetti

FOOD

22 Map p110, B3

It's not cheap but quality costs, and the gourmet delights you'll find here – at what many claim is Rome's best deli – are top of the range. Helpful staff will guide you through the extensive selection that runs the gamut from smelly cheese and homemade pasta to olive oil, vinegar, salami, vegie pies, wine and grappa. You can also order online. (www.volpetti.com; Via Marmorata 47; ⊙8am-2pm & 5-8.15pm Mon-Sat; ⊠Via Marmorata)

MARTIN MOOS/LONELY PLANET IMAGES ©

L'Alibi

Nuovo Mercato di Testaccio

MARKET

23 Map p110, A3

Occupying a new, purpose-built site, Testaccio's market hums with activity as locals go about their daily shopping – picking and prodding the piles of brightly coloured produce, selecting their meat, and cheerfully shouting at all and sundry. (Via Galvani; ⏰6am-3pm Mon-Sat; ⬜Via Marmorata)

Calzature Boccanera

SHOES

24 Map p110, B3

Tatty Testaccio goes glam at this old-fashioned shoe shop. It's lined with just-off-the-runway men's and women's footwear from names such as Fendi, Ferragamo, Prada, D&G and Gucci. There are bags and belts to match and tempting markdowns during the sales. (Via Luca della Robbia 36; ⏰9.30am-1.30pm Tue-Sat, 3.30-7.30pm Mon-Sat; ⬜Via Marmorata)

Local Life
Ostiense & San Paolo

Packed with post-industrial grit, trendy Ostiense is all about cutting-edge clubs, old-school trattorias and slinky new-school bars. The presence of a university campus lends it a buzz and its disued factories provide space for all sorts of after-hours hedonism. Traditional sights are thin on the ground but you will find a fabulous gallery housed in an ex–power plant and the world's third-largest church.

Getting There

Ⓜ **Metro** The best way to access the area. Line B runs to Piramide, Garbatella and Basilica San Paolo.

🚍 **Bus** Take bus 23 or 716 to Via Ostiense.

❶ Coffee & Cakes at Andreotti
Kick-start your day with coffee and cakes at **Andreotti** (Via Ostiense 54; ⊙7.30am-9.30pm; 🚋Via Ostiense), a fashionable cafe-cum-patisserie. Film director and local resident Ferzan Ozpetek is a fan and has been known to cast its *dolci* (sweets) in his films.

❷ Sculpture at Centrale Montemartini
Antiquity meets Fritz Lang's *Metropolis* at the **Centrale Montemartini** (www.centralemontemartini.org; Via Ostiense 106; adult/reduced €6.50/5.50; ⊙9am-7pm Tue-Sun; 🚋Via Ostiense), the striking southern outpost of the Capitoline Museums. In an ex-power plant, ancient Roman sculpture is juxtaposed against diesel engines and giant furnaces. Among the highlights is a youthful *Fanciulla seduta* and 2nd-century-BC *Musa polimnia*.

❸ Garbatella
To experience one of Rome's most idiosyncratic neighbourhoods, make for **Garbatella** (ⓂGarbatella), a charming garden suburb that was developed in the 1920s and '30s to house people who'd been displaced by fascist construction projects in the city centre.

❹ Lunch at Hostaria Zampagna
For a back-to-basics lunch, without any frills or fashionable pretensions, humble **Hostaria Zampagna** (📞06 574 23 06; Via Ostiense 179; meals €25; ⊙Mon-Sat; ⒨Basilica San Paolo) is a neighbourhood stalwart serving good, earthy Roman staples.

❺ Basilica di San Paolo Fuori-le-Mura
The **Basilica di San Paolo Fuori-le-Mura** (www.basilicasanpaolo.org; Via Ostiense 186; ⊙7am-6.30pm; ⒨Basilica San Paolo) is the world's third-largest church. Much of the original basilica was destroyed by fire in 1823 but survivors include the 5th-century triumphal arch, with its heavily restored mosaics, and the Gothic tabernacle.

❻ Aperitif at Doppiozeroo
Early evening is aperitif time, and the place to go is **Doppiozeroo** (www.doppiozeroo.com; Via Ostiense 68; ⊙7am-2am; 🚋Via Ostiense), back to the north near Andreotti. Between 6pm and 9pm, fashion-conscious Romans flock to this urbane modern bar to fill up on pizza slices, couscous, salads and pastas.

❼ Cool Clubbing
Ostiense is serious clubbing country. Via Libetta and Via degli Argonauti form the district's hedonistic hub, where top-notch global DJs dish out anything from nu-house to thumping old-school techno. Big clubs include **Goa** (www.goaclub.com; Via Libetta 13; ⒨Garbatella), **La Saponeria** (www.saponeriaclub.it; Via degli Argonauti 20; ⒨Garbatella) and **Rashomon** (www.rashomonclub.com; Via degli Argonauti 16; ⒨Garbatella).

Explore

Trastevere & Gianicolo

Trastevere, with its lost-in-time laneways and ochre *palazzi* (mansions), is one of Rome's best-looking and most vivacious neighbourhoods. Formerly a bastion of working-class independence, it's now a trendy hang-out full of restaurants, cafes and pubs catering to a cast of tourists, travellers, students and street sellers. Behind it, the Gianicolo hill rises serenely above the maelstrom, offering superb views.

The Sights in a Day

☀️ Start the day by paying homage to St Cecilia, the patron saint of music, at the **Basilica di Santa Cecilia in Trastevere** (p128), and then spying on a saucy Bernini sculpture at the **Chiesa di San Francesco d'Assisi a Ripa** (p128). Suitably inspired, head over to **Piazza Santa Maria in Trastevere** (p125) and the neighbourhood's main must-see, the **Basilica di Santa Maria in Trastevere** (p122). For a final flourish before lunch, continue on to **Villa Farnesina** (p128), a palatial Renaissance villa famed for its Raphael frescoes.

☀️ After lunch at the **Trattoria degli Amici** (p130), retrace your footsteps back to the **Galleria Nazionale d'Arte Antica di Palazzo Corsini** (p129). Afterwards, take an hour or so to chill out in Rome's botanical gardens, the nearby **Orto Botanico** (p129). Recharged, head up the Gianicolo hill to admire Bramante's **Tempietto** (p128) and some superb rooftop views.

🌙 For a real Trastevere night to remember, dine at **Glass Hostaria** (p130) and then take in a gig at **Big Mama** (p125).

 Top Sights

Basilica di Santa Maria in Trastevere (p122)

🔍 **Local Life**

A Night Out in Trastevere (p124)

💜 **Best of Rome**

Eating
Glass Hostaria (p130)

For Free
Gianicolo (p124)

Architecture
Tempietto del Bramante (p128)

Shopping
La Cravatta su Misura (p134)

Antica Caciara Trasteverina (p134)

Porta Portese (p135)

Getting There

🚊 **Tram** Tram 8 from Largo di Torre Argentina runs to the main drag of Viale di Trastevere.

🚌 **Bus** From Termini, bus H runs to Viale di Trastevere. For Gianicolo, if you don't fancy the steep steps from Via Mameli, take bus 870 from Piazza delle Rovere.

Top Sights
Basilica di Santa Maria in Trastevere

This ravishing basilica is said to be the oldest church in Rome dedicated to the Virgin Mary. Dating to the early 3rd century, it was commissioned by Pope Callixtus III on the site where, according to legend, a fountain of oil had miraculously sprung from the ground. The basilica has been much altered over the centuries and its current Romanesque form is the result of a 12th-century revamp. The portico came later, added by Carlo Fontana in 1702.

Map p126, C5

Piazza Santa Maria in Trastevere

admission free

7.30am-9pm

Viale di Trastevere

Don't Miss

The Exterior

Rising above the four papal statues on Domenico Fontana's 18th-century porch, the basilica's restrained 12th-century facade is most notable for its beautiful medieval mosaic. This glittering gold banner depicts Mary feeding Jesus surrounded by 10 women bearing lamps.

Towering above the church is a 12th-century Romanesque bell tower, complete with its very own mosaic – look in the small niche near the top.

The Mosaics

The basilica's main drawcard is its golden 12th-century mosaics. In the apse, look out for the dazzling depiction of Christ and his mother flanked by various saints, and, on the far left, Pope Innocent II holding a model of the church. Beneath this is a series of six mosaics by Pietro Cavallini (c 1291) illustrating the life of the Virgin.

Design Features

The interior boasts a typical 12th-century design with three naves divided by Roman columns, some plundered from the Terme di Caracalla. On the right of the altar, near a spiralling Paschal candlestick, is an inscription, *Fons Olei*, which marks the spot where the miraculous oil fountain supposedly sprung. Up above, the coffered golden ceiling was designed in 1617 by Domenichino.

Cappella Avila

The last chapel on the left, the Cappella Avila, is worth a look for its stunning 17th-century dome. Antonio Gherardi's clever 1680 design depicts four angels holding the circular base of a large lantern whose columns rise to give the effect of a second cupola within a larger outer dome.

☑ Top Tips

▶ Have some coins handy to drop in the light box to illuminate the mosaics.

▶ Avoid visiting during mass, which is held at 9am, 5.30pm and 8.30pm Monday to Friday; 9am, 5.30pm and 8pm Saturday; 8.30am, 10am, 11.30am, 5.30pm and 6.45pm Sunday.

▶ To see the facade in its entirety, step back so you can see above the porch.

✕ Take a Break

Avoid the rip-off tourist traps on the piazza outside. Instead, grab a drink or snack at Ombre Rosse (p133), ideally at one of its street-side tables. Alternatively, grab a slice of pizza from the neighbourhood's historic bakery Forno la Renella (p131).

Local Life
A Night Out in Trastevere

With its enchanting lanes, vibrant piazzas and carnival atmosphere, Trastevere is one of the city's favourite after-dark hang-outs. Foreigners love it, but it's also a local haunt and Romans come here in swaths, particularly on balmy summer nights when street sellers set up camp on the picturesque alleyways and bar crowds spill out onto the streets.

1 Views on the Gianicolo

The early evening is a good time to enjoy the sweeping panoramic views from the Gianicolo. This leafy hill, Rome's highest, was the scene of vicious fighting during Italian unification but is now a tranquil spot. Lap up the vibe with a relaxed drink at the summer art cafe, **Gianicolo 150** (Piazza Giuseppe Garibaldi; ⏰7pm-2am Jun-Sep; 🚌Via del Gianicolo).

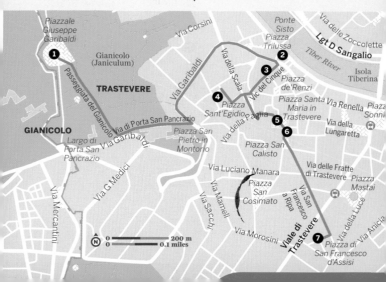

❷ Aperitif at Freni e Frizioni

On a raised piazza near the main riverside road, **Freni e Frizioni** (www.freniefrizioni.com; Via del Politeama 4-6; ⏱6.30pm-2am; 🚋Piazza Trilussa) is an ex-garage – the name means 'brakes and clutches' – turned designer-grunge bar. It pulls in a spritz-loving arty crowd that flocks here to slurp well-priced mojitos and fill up at the popular 7pm *aperitivo*.

❸ Art at Edicola Notte

To take in an exhibition without breaking stride, check out **Edicola Notte** (www.edicolanotte.com; Vicolo del Cinque 23; ⏱8pm-2am; 🚋Piazza Trilussa), Rome's tiniest art gallery. The brainchild of an expat Chinese-Malay artist, it measures a mere 7m by 1m, and stages regular micro-shows by contemporary Italian and international artists.

❹ Dinner at Da Lucia

For a real Trastevere experience, dine beneath fluttering neighbourhood knickers on a hidden cobbled backstreet. **Da Lucia** (📞06 580 36 01; Vicolo del Mattonato 2; meals €30; ⏱Tue-Sun; 🚋Viale di Trastevere) is a terrific trattoria, popular with locals and tourists alike, that serves up a cavalcade of Roman specialities as well as gut-busting antipasti. Cash only.

❺ Hanging Out on Piazza Santa Maria in Trastevere

Trastevere's focal square, **Piazza Santa Maria in Trastevere** (🚋Viale di Trastevere), is a prime people-watching spot. During the day it's full of chatting locals and guidebook-toting tourists but by night the foreign students, young Romans and out-of-towners move in, all on the lookout for a good time. The octagonal fountain is of Roman origin and was restored by Carlo Fontana in 1692.

❻ Drinks at Bar San Calisto

One of the few bars in Trastevere to resist the onset of new trends, **Bar San Calisto** (Piazza San Calisto 3-5; ⏱5.30pm-2am Mon-Sat; 🚋Viale di Trastevere) is a local institution. A motley crew of students, punks, card-playing *nonni* (grandpas) and affected bohemians congregate here for dirt-cheap drinks and the bar's legendary chocolate, drunk hot with cream in winter and licked as gelato in summer.

❼ Blues at Big Mama

To wallow in the Eternal City blues, there's only one place to go – **Big Mama** (📞06 581 25 51; www.bigmama.it; Vicolo di San Francesco a Ripa 18; ⏱9pm-1.30am Tue-Sun Oct–mid-Jun; 🚋Viale di Trastevere), a cramped Trastevere basement. There are weekly residencies from well-known Italian musicians, and frequent blues, jazz, funk, soul and R&B concerts by international artists.

Piazza in Piscinula

Via Lungarina

Via Lungaretta

Via della del'Drago

11

Sonnino Piazza

Via dei Salumi

Via dei Genovesi

24

Basilica di Santa Cecilia in Trastevere **1**

Piazza di Santa Cecilia

Via Anica

Via G Santini

Piazza de' Mercanti

Piazza di San Francesco d'Assisi

27

Via di San Gallicano

Via della Lungaretta

Basilica di Santa Maria in Trastevere

Piazza Santa Maria in Trastevere

Via della Paglia

Via del Porta San Pancrazio

Piazza San Pietro in Montorio

3

Tempietto del Bramante

Via Garibaldi

Via della Frusta

Via G Venzian

Via Luciano Manara

Via dei Fienaroli

20

10

Via delle Fratte di Trastevere

Via Cardinale Marmaggi

Piazza Mastai

Viale di Trastevere

Via San Francesco a Ripa

17

25

14

Via della Luce

Piazza San Francesco d'Assisi

2 Chiesa di San Francesco d'Assisi a Ripa

Via di San Michele

Via Anica

Porta di Ripa Grande

Lgt Aventino

Piazza dell'Emporio

Ponte Sublicio

Largo Ascianghi

26

Piazzale Portuense

23

Piazza Porta Portese

Via Portuense

Largo Ascianghi

Piazza Bernardino da Feltre

Via M Carcani

Via Dandolo

Piazza San Cosimato

Viale Glorioso

Via Morosini

Via F Casini

Via Mameli

19

Via Sacchi

Via Dandolo

Via Calandrelli

Viale Nicola Fabrizi

Villa Sciarra

200 m

0.1 miles

Sights

Basilica di Santa Cecilia in Trastevere

CHURCH

1 Map p126, E6

It was here that St Cecilia (the patron saint of music) was martyred in 230. Below the altar, Stefano Moderno's breathtaking sculpture shows how her miraculously preserved body was found in the Catacombe di San Callisto in 1599. Roman ruins lurk underground, while the nun's choir harbours unmissable fragments of Pietro Cavallini's 13th-century *Last Judgement* fresco. (Piazza di Santa Cecilia; admission basilica/Cavallini fresco/crypt free/€2.50/2.50; ⏱basilica & crypt 9.30am-2.30pm & 4-7.30pm, fresco 10am-2.30pm Mon-Sat; 🚍🚊Viale di Trastevere)

Chiesa di San Francesco d'Assisi a Ripa

CHURCH

2 Map p126, D7

This 17th-century church is home to one of Bernini's raciest sculptures. The *Beata Ludovica Albertoni* (Blessed Ludovica Albertoni; 1674) shows Ludovica, a Franciscan nun, in a state of rapture as she reclines, eyes shut, mouth open, one hand touching her breast. The church sits on the site of a hospice that was visited by St Francis of Assisi in 1219. (Piazza di San Francesco d'Assisi 88; ⏱7am-noon & 2-7.30pm; 🚍🚊Viale di Trastevere)

Tempietto del Bramante

HISTORICAL BUILDING

3 Map p126, A5

Bramante's perfectly proportioned Tempietto (Little Temple) is hidden in the courtyard of the Chiesa di San Pietro in Montorio, reputedly the site of St Peter's crucifixion. Lauded as the first great building of the High Renaissance, it was completed in 1508, with Bernini adding the staircase in 1628. (Piazza San Pietro in Montorio 2; ⏱tempietto 9.30am-12.30pm & 4-6pm Tue-Sun summer, 9.30am-12.30pm & 2-4.30pm Tue-Sun winter, church 8.30am-noon & 3-4pm Mon-Fri, 9.30am-12.30pm & 2-4.30pm Tue-Sun; 🚍Via Garibaldi)

Villa Farnesina

PALAZZO

4 Map p126, B3

This luxurious 16th-century palace was designed by Sienese architect Baldassare Peruzzi who, along with Sebastiano del Piombo and Raphael, smothered the place in frescoes. While Raphael painted the *Triumph of Galatea*, he did little more than design the celebrated *Cupid and Psyche*; it was executed by his assistants while he dallied with his mistress from a nearby bakery. (www.villafarnesina.it; Via della Lungara 230; adult/reduced €5/4; ⏱9am-5pm Mon, Sat & 2nd Sun of month, 10am-2pm Tue-Fri; 🚍Lungotevere della Farnesina)

Villa Farnesina

Galleria Nazionale d'Arte Antica di Palazzo Corsini

GALLERY

5 ◎ Map p126, B3

Once home to Queen Christina of Sweden, whose richly frescoed bedroom witnessed a steady stream of male and female lovers, 16th-century Palazzo Corsini houses part of Italy's national art collection. Scan the walls for Van Dyck's *Madonna della paglia* (Madonna of the Straw), Rubens' *St Sebastian* and Caravaggio's *San Giovanni Battista* (St John the Baptist). (www.galleriaborghese.it; Via della Lungara 10; adult/reduced €5/2.50; ⊙8.30am-7.30pm Tue-Sun; ⌂Lungotevere della Farnesina)

Orto Botanico

BOTANICAL GARDEN

6 ◎ Map p126, A3

Established in 1883, Rome's 12-hectare botanical gardens are a soothing antidote to the capital's urban excess. Chill out under the dizzying palms; check out the healing Giardino dei Semplici (a garden with 300 species of medicinal plants); smell your way through the Giardino degli Aromi (labelled in Braille); or simply fall for the dreamy city views. (Largo Cristina di Svezia 24; adult/reduced €8/4; ⊙9am-5.30pm Mon-Sat winter, to 6.30pm summer; ⌂Lungotevere della Farnesina)

Galleria Lorcan O'Neill

GALLERY

7 Map p126, A1

Kick-started by a London art dealer and set in a converted stable, this is one of Rome's most respected private galleries. It features regular exhibitions by exponents of diverse styles and mediums – think Tracey Emin and Max Rental – as well as works by local talents such as Luigi Ontani and Pietro Ruffo. (www.lorcanoneill.com; Via degli Orti d'Alibert 1e; admission free; ☉noon-8pm Mon-Fri, 2-8pm Sat; 🚊Lungotevere Gianicolense)

Eating

Sabatinos

Glass Hostaria

MODERN ITALIAN €€€

8 Map p126, B4

Trastevere's foremost foodie address, the Glass Hostaria exudes contemporary cool with its sophisticated, modernist interior and artful food. Chef Cristina Bowerman's refined menu includes high-class Italian fare and more innovative dishes peppered with Japanese flavours and tropical spices. Go à la carte or opt for one of two tasting menus – with five (€70) or seven (€90) courses. (☎06 5833 5903; www.glass-restaurant.it; Vicolo del Cinque 58; meals €70-80; ☉8-11.30pm Tue-Sun; 🚊Lungotevere della Farnesina)

Trattoria degli Amici

TRADITIONAL ITALIAN €€

9 Map p126, B4

Boasting a prime location on a pretty piazza, this cheerful trattoria is run by a local charity and staffed by volunteers and people with disabilities, who welcome guests with a warmth not always apparent in this touristy neck of the woods. And with its outside tables, it's a lovely place to dig into fresh, well-prepared Italian classics and enjoy the neighbourhood atmosphere. (☎06 580 60 33; Piazza Sant'Egidio 6; meals €30; ☉closed Sun dinner; 🚊🚌Viale di Trastevere)

Paris

TRADITIONAL ITALIAN €€€

10 Map p126, C5

Named after its founder, not the French capital, this elegant, old-fashioned restaurant is the best place outside of the ghetto to tuck into Jewish-Roman food. Perennial crowd-pleasers include *fritto misto con bac-*

calà (deep-fried vegetables with salted cod), *carciofi alla giudia* (Jewish-style artichokes) and just-right *rigatoni alla carbonara* (pasta with egg and bacon sauce). (✆06 581 53 78; www.ristorante paris.com; Piazza San Calisto 7; meals €50; ☺lunch & dinner Tue-Sat, lunch Sun; 🚊🚊Viale di Trastevere)

La Gensola SEAFOOD €€

11 Map p126, E5

In Trastevere's slightly quieter eastern half, this classy yet unpretentious trattoria thrills diners with its delicious Sicilian-inspired food and top-quality seafood. Star turns include *spaghetti ai ricci di mare freschi* (with fresh sea urchins), linguine with fresh anchovies and *pecorino* cheese, and fried *zuccherini* (tiny fish) with fresh mint. (✆06 581 63 12; www.osteriagensola.it; Piazza della Gensola 15; meals €50; ☺closed Sun summer; 🚊🚊Viale di Trastevere)

Dar Poeta PIZZERIA €

12 Map p126, B4

This much-loved pizzeria is tucked down an attractive side-street just metres from the action. Loud and always busy, it serves up a bustling, cheery atmosphere and hearty wood-fired pizzas that fall somewhere between classic wafer-thin Roman pizzas and the softer, doughier Neapolitan versions. Expect queues. (✆06 588 05 16; Vicolo del Bologna 46; pizzas from €6; 🚊Lungotevere della Farnesina)

Bir & Fud PIZZERIA €

13 Map p126, B4

Boutique Italian beers and top-notch, simple flavours define this lively pizzeria. Join the fans for *supplì* (crunchy rice croquettes) and bubbling thin-crust pizza, dished out by clued-up staff who'll find you the perfect brew to wash it all down with. Book ahead. (✆06 589 40 16; Via Benedetta 23; meals €25; ☺7.30pm-midnight, to 2am Fri & Sat; 🚊Lungotevere della Farnesina)

Sisini PIZZA AL TAGLIO €

14 Map p126, C6

Locals know where to come for the best sliced pizza in Trastevere, and you'll need to jostle with them to make it to the counter. Simple varieties reign supreme – try the *margherita* (tomatoes, basil and mozzarella) or *zucchine* (zucchini) and you'll see what we mean. (Via San Francesco a Ripa 137; ☺9am-10.30pm Mon-Sat; 🚊🚊Viale di Trastevere)

Forno la Renella PIZZA AL TAGLIO €

15 Map p126, C4

The wood-fired ovens at this historic neighbourhood bakery have been firing for decades, producing daily batches of pizza, bread and biscuits. Pizza toppings (and fillings) vary seasonally, pleasing fans who span skinheads with bulldogs to chihuahua-clutching pensioners. (Via del Moro 15-16; pizza slices from €2.50; ☺7am-2am Tue-Sat, to 10pm Sun & Mon; 🚊Lungotevere della Farnesina)

Understand

Aperitivo

- -

Hit many of the capital's bars in the early evening and you'll find crowds of animated Romans chatting over cocktails and plates of finger food. Welcome to *l'ora d'aperitivo* – happy hour, Roman-style. The *aperitivo*, a nightly ritual imported from the northern cities of Milan and Turin, is basically a souped-up bar buffet served between about 6pm and 9pm. The way it works is that you order your drink – there's usually a standard charge of €8 to €10 – and tuck into the buffet. Simple.

Classic Drinks

Most bars offer a decent selection of Italian wines and a limited choice of cocktails. But for a classic *aperitivo* tipple you should go for a negroni, made with Campari, red vermouth and gin; an Americano, a mix of Campari, red vermouth and soda; or a spritz, made from Aperol or Campari and *prosecco* sparkling wine.

The Buffet

Where in the past you might have been served a bowl of olives and salty nuts, now bars go all out to impress with their lavish buffet displays. These vary from place to place, and some bars have their own specialities, but a typical spread might include olive-stuffed pastries, bite-sized frittatas, pasta salads, mini-pizzas, bowls of spicy couscous, steaming risottos, grilled vegetables, cheeses and cold cuts. Play your cards right and you might well find you've had dinner for little more than the price of a drink. But while it may be tempting to pile that plate sky high, don't forget that this is the land of *la bella figura*, where looking cool is good, and canapé landslides are not. Do like the locals do and stuff yourself silly *discreetly*.

Top Spots

For a classy fill-up, don't miss the Med-Arabesque spread at hit Trastevere haunt Freni e Frizioni (p125) or the rich banquet laid on by the fashionable Ostiense bar Doppiozeroo (p119). The historic Pigneto hang-out Necci (p93) offers a relaxed bohemian atmosphere while ever-eclectic Micca Club (p89) dishes out tunes and fine cocktails.

Drinking

Ma Che Siete Venuti a Fà BAR

16 Map p126, C3

Named after a football chant, which translates politely as: 'What did you come here for?', this pint-sized place is a beer-buff's paradise, packing in a huge number of artisanal beers, including the caramel-like tipple Italiano Bibock (by Birrificio Italiano) and some oddly named Danish and Belgian numbers – anyone for a bottle of 'Cat's Piss'? (Via Benedetta 25; ⊙11am-2am; ⊠Lungotevere della Farnesina)

Babylon Cafe BAR

17 Map p126, C6

A contemporary bar serving everything from cappuccino and tea to ice cream, aperitifs and late-night cocktails. It heaves at lunchtime as crowds of clued-up Romans flock to fill up on the daily buffet spread. But it's also a lively evening hang-out pulling in punters for the daily *aperitivo* (7pm to 10pm) and occasional live music. (Via San Francesco a Ripa 151; ⊙6am-2am; ⊠⊠Viale di Trastevere)

Ombre Rosse WINE BAR

18 Map p126, B4

Warm wooden interiors, a piazza-side location and cosmopolitan crowds lend much-loved Ombre Rosse effortless continental cool. There's a fine selection of rums and whiskies, a full food menu and live jazz/blues/acoustic on Thursday evenings from September to April. (www.ombrerossecaffe.it; Piazza Sant'Egidio 12; ⊙8am-2am Mon-Sat, 11am-2am Sun; ⊠⊠Viale di Trastevere)

Il Baretto BAR

19 Map p126, B6

A steep climb up Via Garibaldi, this smooth cocktail bar is a picture with its floor-to-ceiling panoramic windows, vintage-meets-pop-art aesthetic and glossy, good-looking clientele. Add meaty basslines and you have the recipe for a fashionable night out. (Via Garibaldi 27; ⊙6am-2am Mon-Sat, 5pm-2am Sun; ⊠Via Garibaldi)

Libreria del Cinema CAFE

20 Map p126, C5

Ponder Pasolini over peppermint tea at this intimate cafe, set snugly inside a cinema bookshop. In an atmosphere filled with the chatter of local directors, actors and writers, the bookshop itself boasts an arty selection of DVDs, as well as a busy cultural calendar. Check the website for upcoming screenings, readings and discussions. (www.libreriadelcinema.roma.it; Via dei Fienaroli 31; ⊙4-10pm Mon-Fri, to 11pm Sat, 2-9pm Sun; ⊠⊠⊠Viale di Trastevere)

La Mescita WINE BAR

21 Map p126, C4

One for aficionados, this snug wine bar sits inside the entrance to the upmarket restaurant Enoteca Ferrara. It lays on a fantastic *aperitivo* spread and has an encyclopedic wine list with about 35 labels available by the glass. (Piazza Trilussa 41; ⊙6pm-2am; ⎙Lungotevere della Farnesina)

Entertainment

Lettere Caffè   LIVE MUSIC

 Map p126, D7

Culture vultures call into Lettere to flick through books, schmooze over drinks and catch the eclectic, arty line-up. Expect regular live gigs, poetry slams, comedy and gay nights, followed by DJ sets playing indie and new wave. Scan the website for upcoming gigs. (www.letterecaffe.org; Via San Francesco a Ripa 100-1; ⊙7pm-2am; ⎙⎙Viale di Trastevere)

Nuovo Sacher   CINEMA

23 ⭐ Map p126, D8

Owned by cult Roman film director Nanni Moretti, this retro cinema is the place to catch the latest European arthouse flick. Originally designed to support home-grown film talent, it occasionally shows films in their original language (English, French, Swedish etc). Summer screenings take place in the courtyard next to the cinema. (✆06 581 81 16; www.sacherfilm.eu; Largo Ascianghi 1; ⎙⎙Viale di Trastevere)

Shopping

La Cravatta su Misura   ACCESSORIES

24 🔒 Map p126, E6

With ties draped over the wooden furniture and rolls of fine Italian silks lined up out back, this inviting shop is a throwback to a smarter era. La Cravatta makes exquisite neckwear and to customer specifications and, at a push, can do you a tie in a few hours. There are also scarves available from €25. (www.lacravattasumisura.it; Via Santa Cecilia 12; ⊙10am-7pm Mon-Sat; ⎙⎙Viale di Trastevere)

Antica Caciara Trasteverina   FOOD, WINE

25 🔒 Map p126, C6

The fresh ricotta is a prized possession at this century-old deli, and usually snapped up by lunch. If you're too late, take solace in the famous *pecorino romano* or the *burrata pugliese* (a creamy cheese from the Puglia region), or simply lust after the fragrant hams, bread, *baccalà* (salted cod), peppers, Sicilian anchovies and local wines. (Via San Francesco a Ripa 140; ⊙7am-2pm & 4-8pm Mon-Sat; ⎙⎙Viale di Trastevere)

Porta Portese   MARKET

26 Map p126, D8

Locals joke that if you have something stolen during the week, you can buy it back here on Sunday. Rome's biggest, busiest and best-known flea market has thousands of stalls pushing everything from cheap jeans, shoes and bags to rare books, Peruvian ponchos, iPods and the odd kitchen sink. Keep your valuables safe and don't forget to haggle. (Piazza Porta Portese; ⏰7am-1pm Sun; 🚌🚊Viale di Trastevere)

Roma-Store   PERFUME

27 Map p126, D5

On the main pedestrian strip through Trastevere, this unmarked perfume shop is crammed full of deliciously enticing scents and lotions. Get fresh with in-the-know brands such as Serge Lutens, Laboratorio Olfattivo, E Coudray and État Libre, or stick with classics English Floris and Italian Aqua di Parma. (Via della Lungaretta 63; ⏰10am-8pm; 🚌🚊Viale di Trastevere)

Joseph Debach   SHOES

28 Map p126, C4

Footwear becomes art at the tiny boutique of Libyan-born designer Joseph Debach. Shoes with teeth and tongues, covered in cartoon collages or funked-up with an abacus wedge heel? These

WILL SALTER/LONELY PLANET IMAGES ©

Porta Portese

outrageous numbers are more about 'wow' than 'wear' but they're quite a sight. (Vicolo del Cinque 19; ⏰from 7.30pm Sat-Thu; 🚌Lungotevere della Farnesina)

Scala Quattordici   FASHION

29 Map p126, B4

Make yourself over à la Audrey Hepburn at this classic Trastevere boutique. It's filled with haughty attitude, rolls of luscious fabrics and exquisite off-the-peg and tailor-made outfits. (Via della Scala 13-14; 🚌Lungotevere della Farnesina)

Explore

Vatican City & Prati

The Vatican, the world's smallest sovereign state (0.44 sq km), sits over the river from the *centro storico* (historic centre). Centred on the domed St Peter's Basilica, it's a spiritual, artistic and touristic superpower, home to some of the world's most famous works of art and hundreds of overpriced restaurants and souvenir shops. It's busy by day but at night the action shifts to the restaurants and trattorias in nearby Prati.

The Sights in a Day

☀ Brace yourself for the day ahead with a couple of still-warm pastries from **Dolce Maniera** (p152). Thus charged, head off to the **Vatican Museums** (p142) to explore one of the world's greatest art collections. You'll never see everything in one go, but be sure to check out the **Cortile Ottagono** (p145), the **Stanze di Raffaello** (Raphael Rooms; p145) and, of course, the **Sistine Chapel** (p143). Afterwards, reflect on what you've seen over a light lunch at **Del Frate** (p152).

☀ After lunch, head to **Piazza San Pietro** (p150), the dramatic gateway to **St Peter's Basilica** (p138), the Vatican's imperious showcase church. Explore the awe-inspiring marble-clad interior and climb the dome before heading down Via della Conciliazione to round off the afternoon at the landmark **Castel Sant'Angelo** (p150).

☾ Come evening, treat yourself to some high-quality Roman cuisine at **L'Arcangelo** (p151) before retiring to jazz mecca **Alexanderplatz** (p153) to see out the day with a concert.

👁 Top Sights

St Peter's Basilica (p138)

Vatican Museums (p142)

❤ Best of Rome

Architecture

St Peter's Basilica (p138)

Piazza San Pietro (p150)

Museums

Vatican Museums (p142)

Castel Sant'Angelo (p150)

Eating

Pizzarium (p150)

Gelarmony (p150)

L'Arcangelo (p151)

Getting There

Ⓜ **Metro** Take metro line A to Ottaviano-San Pietro.

🚌 **Bus** From Termini, bus 40 is the quickest option – it'll drop you off near Castel Sant'Angelo. Bus 64 covers a similar route but stops more often. Bus 492 runs to Piazza del Risorgimento from Stazione Tiburtina, passing through Piazza Barberini and the *centro storico*.

Top Sights
St Peter's Basilica

In a city of outstanding churches, none can hold a candle to St Peter's Basilica (Basilica di San Pietro), Italy's biggest, richest and most spectacular cathedral. The current church, the world's second largest (after the Basilica of Our Lady of Peace in Yamoussoukro, Ivory Coast), was built over the original 4th-century basilica and completed in 1626 after 150 years of construction. It contains some brilliant works of art, including three of Rome's most celebrated masterpieces: Michelangelo's *Pietà*, his breathtaking dome, and Bernini's baldachin (canopy) over the papal altar.

👁 Map p148, C4

Piazza San Pietro

admission free

🕑 7am-7pm Apr-Sep, to 6.30pm Oct-Mar

Ⓜ Ottaviano-San Pietro

Dome detail

Don't Miss

The Facade

Completed in 1612, Carlo Maderno's immense facade features eight 27m-high columns and 13 statues representing Christ, St John the Baptist and the 11 apostles. The central balcony, known as the Loggia della Benedizione, is where the pope stands to deliver his Christmas and Easter blessing. In the grand atrium, the first door on the right is the **Porta Santa** (Holy Door), which is only opened in Jubilee years.

Pietà

At the beginning of the right aisle, Michelangelo's hauntingly beautiful *Pietà* sits in its own chapel behind a panel of bullet-proof glass. Sculpted when he was a little-known 25-year-old (in 1499), it's the only work he ever signed – his signature is etched into the sash across the Madonna's breast.

Baldachin

Dominating the centre of the basilica is Bernini's 29m-high baldachin. Supported by four spiral columns and made with bronze taken from the Pantheon, it stands over the **papal altar**, which itself sits on the site of St Peter's grave. In front, the elaborate **Confessione**, built by Carlo Maderno, is where St Peter was originally buried.

Monument to Alexander VII

To the left of the baldachin is one of the basilica's most dramatic works, the monument to Alexander VII. Featuring a billowing marble drape held aloft by a creepy bronze skeleton with an hourglass in its hand, this was Bernini's last work in the basilica, completed in 1678.

☑ Top Tips

▶ Dress appropriately if you want to get in – no shorts, miniskirts or bare shoulders.

▶ Free English-language tours are run from the Centro Servizi Pellegrini e Turisti at 9.45am Tuesday and Thursday, and 2.15pm daily Monday to Friday.

▶ Queues are inevitable at the security checks, but they move quickly.

▶ Lines are generally shorter during lunch hours and late afternoon.

▶ Be aware that pickpockets operate in the Vatican, so keep watch of your valuables.

✗ Take a Break

Avoid the tourist traps around the basilica and head to nearby Prati. For a sinful snack, stop off at the Sicilian gelateria and pastry shop Gelarmony (p150), while for something more substantial, enjoy a traditional trattoria lunch at Hostaria Dino & Tony (p151).

Cattedra di San Pietro

Behind the altar in the tribune at the end of the basilica, the **throne of St Peter** (1665) is the centrepiece of Bernini's extraordinary Cattedra di San Pietro. In the middle of the elaborate gilded-bronze throne, supported by statues of saints, is a wooden seat, which was once thought to have been St Peter's but in fact dates to the 9th century.

Dome

Above the baldachin, Michelangelo's dome rises to a height of 119m. Based on Brunelleschi's cupola in Florence, it's supported by four stone piers named after the saints whose statues adorn their Bernini-designed niches – Longinus, Helena, Veronica and Andrew. To climb the **dome** (with/without lift €7/5; ☉8am-6pm Apr-Sep, to 5pm Oct-Mar), head to the entrance to the right of the basilica.

Statue of St Peter

At the base of the Pier of St Longinus is a much-loved bronze statue of St Peter, whose right foot has been worn down by centuries of caresses. It is believed to be a 13th-century work by Arnolfo di Cambio. On the Feast Day of St Peter and St Paul (29 June), the statue is dressed in papal robes.

Stuart Monuments

One of the few monuments in the basilica not commemorating a pope,

St Peter's Basilica

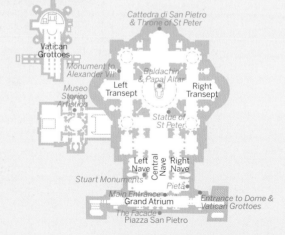

Cattedra di San Pietro & Throne of St Peter

Vatican Grottoes

Monument to Alexander VII

Museo Storico Artistico

Baldachin & Papal Altar

Left Transept

Right Transept

Statue of St Peter

Left Nave

Central Nave

Right Nave

Stuart Monuments

Pietà

Main Entrance
Grand Atrium

Entrance to Dome & Vatican Grottoes

The Façade
Piazza San Pietro

Understand
Christina, Queen of Sweden

On a pillar just beyond Michelangelo's *Pietà* is Carlo Fontana's monument to Queen Christina of Sweden, a woman whose reputation was far from holy. Famously portrayed by Greta Garbo in the 1933 film *Queen Christina*, the Swedish monarch is one of only three women buried in the basilica – the other two are Queen Charlotte of Cyprus, a minor 15th-century royal, and Agnesina Colonna, a 16th-century Italian aristocrat. Christina earned her place by abdicating the Swedish throne and converting to Catholicism in 1655. As Europe's most high-profile convert, she became a Vatican favourite and spent much of her later life in Rome, where she enjoyed fame as a brilliant patron of the arts. Her active private life was the subject of much salacious gossip and rumours abounded of affairs with courtiers and acquaintances of both sexes.

Antonio Canova's vaguely erotic white marble tablet is dedicated to the last three members of the Stuart clan – James Francis Edward Stuart and his two sons, Bonnie Prince Charlie and Henry – the pretenders to the English throne who died in exile in Rome.

Museo Storico Artistico

Accessed from halfway down the left nave, the **Museo Storico Artistico** (adult/reduced €6/4; ⊙8am-7pm Apr-Sep, to 6.15pm Oct-Mar) showcases the basilica's sacred relics and priceless artefacts. Highlights include a tabernacle by Donatello; the Colonna Santa, a 4th-century Byzantine column from the earlier church; and the 6th-century *Crux vaticana* (Vatican Cross), a gift from the emperor Justinian II.

Vatican Grottoes

Extending beneath the basilica, the **Vatican Grottoes** (admission free; ⊙8am-6pm Apr-Sep, to 5.30pm Oct-Mar) were created during the construction of the current basilica in the late 16th century as a burial place for popes. You'll see many papal tombs as well as several huge columns from the original 4th-century basilica.

Tomb of St Peter

Excavations beneath the basilica have uncovered part of the original church and what archaeologists believe is the **Tomb of St Peter** (admission €13). The excavations can only be visited by people over 15 on a 90-minute guided tour. To book a spot email the **Ufficio Scavi** (Excavations Office; ☎06 6988 5318; scavi@fsp.va), as far in advance as possible.

Top Sights
Vatican Museums

Visiting the Vatican Museums (Musei Vaticani) is a thrilling and unforgettable experience. The highlight is the Michelangelo-decorated Sistine Chapel, but with some 7km of exhibitions and more masterpieces than many small countries, there's enough art on display to keep you busy for years – it's said that if you spent one minute on every exhibit it would take you 12 years to see everything. Housing it all is the 5.5-hectare Palazzo Apostolico Vaticano, which also serves as the pope's official residence.

👁 Map p148, C3

📞 06 6988 4676

http://mv.vatican.va

Viale Vaticano

adult/reduced €16/8

🕘 9am-6pm Mon-Sat, ticket office closes 4pm

Ⓜ Ottaviano-San Pietro

Spiral staircase (p147)

Don't Miss

Sistine Chapel

Named after Pope Sixtus IV, the 15th-century Sistine Chapel (Cappella Sistina) is home to two of the world's most famous works of art – Michelangelo's ceiling frescoes and his *Giudizio universale*. It also serves an important religious function as the chapel where the papal conclave meets to elect a new pope.

Sistine Chapel Ceiling Frescoes

Painted between 1508 and 1512, the 800-sq-m frescoes represent nine scenes from the book of Genesis. The most famous panel is the *Creation of Adam*, which shows God pointing his index figure at Adam, thus bringing him to life. Framing the scenes are muscular *ignudi* (athletic male nudes).

Sistine Chapel, Giudizio Universale

Covering the Sistine Chapel's 200-sq-m west wall, Michelangelo's highly charged *Giudizio universale* (Last Judgment; 1535–41) depicts the souls of the dead being torn from their graves to face the wrath of God. When it was unveiled, its swirling mass of naked bodies caused controversy – Pope Pius IV later had Daniele da Volterra add fig leaves and loincloths.

Sistine Chapel Wall Frescoes

Part of the original chapel decoration, the frescoes were painted between 1481 and 1482 by a crack team of Renaissance artists, including Botticelli, Ghirlandaio, Pinturicchio, Perugino and Luca Signorelli. They represent events in the lives of Moses (to the left, looking at the *Giudizio universale*) and Christ (to the right).

☑ Top Tips

▶ The museums are free on the last Sunday of the month, from 9am to 2pm.

▶ To avoid queues, book tickets and guided tours online at http://biglietteriamusei.vatican.va/musei/tickets/do.

▶ Time your visit to minimise waiting: Wednesday mornings are good; the afternoon is better than the morning; avoid Mondays, when many other museums are shut.

▶ The *Guide to the Vatican Museums and City* (€12) is a sound investment, as exhibits are not well labelled.

✖ Take a Break

There's a self-service restaurant and bar near the Pinacoteca, and another bar on the stairs to the Sistine Chapel. But for a real taste to remember, leave the museums and head to Pizzarium (p150), one of Rome's best *pizza al taglio* (pizza by the slice) joints.

Vatican Museums

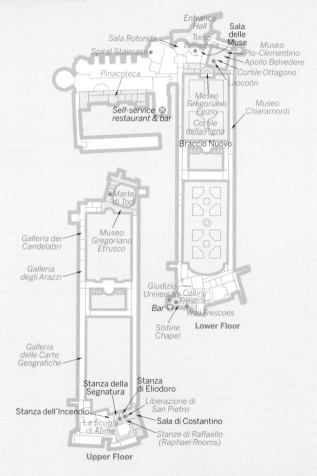

Entrance Hall

Sala delle Muse

Sala Rotonda

Torso Belvedere

Museo Pio-Clementino

Spiral Staircase

Apollo Belvedere

Cortile Ottagono

Pinacoteca

Laocoön

Museo Gregoriano Egizio

Museo Chiaramonti

Self-service restaurant & bar

Cortile della Pigna

Braccio Nuovo

Marte di Todi

Museo Gregoriano Etrusco

Galleria dei Candelabri

Galleria degli Arazzi

Giudizio Universale Ceiling Frescoes

Bar

Wall Frescoes

Galleria delle Carte Geografiche

Sistine Chapel

Lower Floor

Stanza della Segnatura

Stanza di Eliodoro

Liberazione di San Pietro

Stanza dell'Incendio

Sala di Costantino

La Scuola di Atene

Stanze di Raffaello (Raphael Rooms)

Upper Floor

Stanze di Raffaello (Raphael Rooms)

These four frescoed rooms were Pope Julius II's private apartment suite. But while they carry Raphael's name, he only actually painted two – the **Stanza della Segnatura** (Study; 1508–11) and the **Stanza di Eliodoro** (Waiting Room; 1512–14). The **Stanza dell'Incendio** (Dining Room; 1514–17) and the **Sala di Costantino** (Reception Room; 1517–24) were decorated by students following his designs.

Stanze di Raffaello, La Scuola di Atene

Of the frescoes in the Raphael Rooms, the greatest is *The School of Athens* in the Stanza della Segnatura. Depicting scholars gathered around Plato and Aristotle, it includes some notable portraits – the figure in front of the steps is believed to be Michelangelo, Plato's face is supposedly da Vinci's, and the second figure from the right is Raphael himself.

Stanze di Raffaello, Liberazione di San Pietro

The second of the Raphael Rooms, the Stanza di Eliodoro is named for the *Cacciata d'eliodoro* (Expulsion of Heliodorus from the Temple), but for sheer technical bravado, nothing can surpass Raphael's masterly depiction of light in the *Liberation of St Peter*.

Museo Pio-Clementino, Cortile Ottagono

This octagonal courtyard located in the heart of the spectacular Museo Pio-Clementino contains some of the Vatican Museums' finest classical statuary, including the peerless **Apollo belvedere**, a Roman copy of a 4th-century-BC Greek bronze depicting the sun god Apollo, and the 1st-century **Laocoön**, representing a muscular Trojan priest and his two sons in mortal struggle with two sea serpents.

Museo Pio-Clementino, Torso Belvedere

Another of the Museo Pio-Clementino's must-sees is the *Torso belvedere* in the **Sala delle Muse** (Room of the Muses). A fragment of a muscular Greek sculpture from the 1st century BC, it was found in Campo de' Fiori and used by Michelangelo as a model for his *ignudi* in the Sistine Chapel.

Museo Pio-Clementino, Sala Rotonda

This round room contains a number of colossal statues, including the gilded-bronze figure of an odd-looking **Ercole** (Hercules), and an exquisite floor mosaic. The enormous **basin** in the centre of the room was found at Nero's Domus Aurea and is made out of a single piece of red porphyry stone.

Pinacoteca

Often overlooked by visitors, the papal picture gallery boasts Raphael's last work, **La trasfigurazione** (1517–20), and paintings by Giotto, Bellini, Caravaggio, Fra Angelico, Filippo Lippi, Guido Reni, Van Dyck, Pietro da Cortona and Leonardo da Vinci, whose

Understand

The Vatican – a Potted History

Established under the terms of the 1929 Lateran Treaty, the Vatican is the modern vestige of the Papal States, the papal fiefdom that ruled Rome and much of central Italy until Italian unification in 1861. It's an independent nation and as such has a head of state (the pope), government and army (the nattily dressed Swiss Guards).

The Early Days

The Vatican's association with Christianity dates to the 1st century, when St Peter was crucified upside down in Nero's Circus (where Piazza San Pietro now stands). To commemorate this, the 4th-century emperor Constantine commissioned a basilica to be built on the site where the saint was buried.

For centuries, St Peter's Basilica (p138) stood at the centre of a densely populated quarter, later enclosed by Leo IV's Leonine Walls, but it wasn't until the 12th century that the Palazzo Apostolico Vaticano was built. Originally, this served as a temporary shelter – the pope's main residence was Palazzo del Laterano – but, like much of the Vatican, it fell into disrepair during the exile of the papacy to Avignon (1305–78) and the Great Schism (the period between 1378 and 1417 when rival popes ruled in Rome and Avignon).

Later Developments

Life returned to the Vatican in the 16th-century Renaissance, when St Peter's was revamped and the Palazzo Apostolico Vaticano was modernised. The baroque 17th century saw the laying of Piazza San Pietro (p150). However, by this time the papal court had once again upped sticks and settled into Palazzo del Quirinale (p71), where it stayed until 1870.

Controversial Popes

Over the centuries the Vatican has been no stranger to scandal. One of the most controversial pontiffs was Alexander VI (r 1492–1503), the corrupt, nepotistic head of the Borgia family whose eldest son, Cesare, was supposedly the model for Machiavelli's *Prince*. More recently, Pope Pius XIII (r 1939–58) attracted heated criticism for not speaking out against the Nazi persecution of the Jews in WWII.

San Gerolamo (St Jerome; c 1480) was never finished.

Museo Gregoriano Egizio

Founded by Pope Gregory XVI in 1839, this museum contains pieces taken from Egypt in Roman times. The collection is small but there are fascinating exhibits, including the **Trono di rameses II**, part of a statue of the seated king, vividly painted sarcophagi dating from around 1000 BC, and some macabre mummies.

Cortile della Pigna

One of three internal courtyards, the Cortile della Pigna takes its name from the huge Augustan-era bronze pine cone that sits in the courtyard's great niche. In the centre, the 4m-diameter ball, the *Sfera*, is by Italian sculptor Arnaldo Pomodoro.

Museo Chiaramonti

Occupying the long corridor that runs down the lower east flank of the Belvedere Palace, this museum boasts thousands of statues representing everything from immortal gods to playful cherubs to ugly Roman patricians. In the **Braccio Nuovo** (New Wing), look out for the famous statue depicting the Nile as a reclining god covered by 16 babies.

Museo Gregoriano Etrusco, Marte di Todi

The 4th-century-BC *Marte di todi* (Mars of Todi), a full-length bronze of a warrior, is the star of the Museo Gregoriano

Etrusco. On the upper level of the Belvedere Palace, the museum contains artefacts from the Etruscan tombs of northern Lazio, as well as a collection of Greek vases and Roman antiquities.

Galleria dei Candelabri & Galleria degli Arazzi

Originally an open loggia, the Galleria dei Candelabri is packed with classical sculpture and several elegantly carved marble candelabras that give the gallery its name. The corridor continues through to the Galleria degli Arazzi (Tapestry Gallery) and its 10 huge tapestries. The best tapestries, those on the left, were woven in Brussels in the 16th century.

Galleria delle Carte Geografiche

One of the unsung heroes of the Vatican Museums, the 120m-long Map Gallery is hung with 40 huge topographical maps. They were all created between 1580 and 1583 for Pope Gregory XIII, and based on drafts by Ignazio Danti, one of the leading cartographers of his day.

Spiral Staircase

One of the most photographed works in the Vatican Museums is the spiral staircase that you take to exit the complex. The work of architect Giuseppe Moma, it was made in 1932 and served as the museums' main entrance until 2000. In fact, it is actually two staircases incorporated into a single double-helix structure, just like the human DNA strand.

For reviews see

◉	Top Sights	p138
◉	Sights	p150
✖	Eating	p150
◐	Drinking	p152
★	Entertainment	p153
⊕	Shopping	p153

0   500 m
0   0.25 miles

Via Morin
Via della Giuliana
Via Bettolo
Via Camo
Via Barletta
10
Largo Trionfale
Via Otranto
9
Via Andrea Doria
Ottaviano San Pietro
Via Famagosta
7
Via Ostia
Via Leone IV
15
Via Tunisi
Via Candia
Via Ottaviano
Via Cipro
Circonvallazione Trionfale
Cipro-Musei Vaticani
Ⓜ
Via Vespasiano
Via della Meloria
4
Piazza del Risorgimento
Viale Vaticano
Entrance to Vatican Museums
Viale della Zitella
Via della Posta
Borgo Angelico
Vatican Museums ◉
Borgo Vittor
18
VATICAN CITY (CITTÀ DEL VATICANO)
Via del Belvedere
Piazza della Città Leonina
Vatican Gardens
Largo San Martino
Piazza San Pietro
St Peter's Basilica ◉
Centro Servizi Pellegrini e Turisti ⓘ
1
Piazza Pio XII
Piazza dei P Romani
Piazza Santa Marta
Via del Sant'Uffizio
Via Paolo VI
Borgo Sant Spirito
Piazza di Sant'Uffizio
Via Aurelia
Gianicolo (Janiculum
Via Aurelia
Via di Porta Cavalleggeri

PRATI

E **F** **G** **H**

Viale delle Milizie

Via Lepanto

Via Vigliena

Via Fornovo

Ponte
P Nenni

1

Via C A Dalla Chiesa

Via Damiata

Lepanto Ⓜ

Via Farnese

Viale Giulio Cesare

Via Duilio

Via degli Scipioni

Via Pompeo Magno

Ponte
Margherita

Via Caio Mario

Via Emilio

Via Ezio

Via Marcantonio Colonna

Via dei Gracchi

Via Virginio Orsini

Piazza
della
Libertà

Piazza dei
Quiriti

✕ 11

Via Fabio Massimo

✕ 5

Via Germanico

Via dei Gracchi

🚉 12

Via Cola di Rienzo

Via Valadier

Via Ennio Quirini Visconti

Lgt dei Mellini

Via Catullo

Via A Regolo

Via Plinio

Via Orazio

Via Tacito

Via Cicerone

17
🔒

Via Gioachino
Belli

Via Varrone

19
🔒

16
⭐

Via Propertio

Via Tibullo

Via Terenzio

Via Boezio

Via Della Valle

Via Cassiodoro

✕ 6

Via Lucrezio Caro

Via Pietro Cossa

Via S Porcari

🚉13

Via Cancellieri

Via Crescenzio

Via Marianna Dionigi

Via Alberico II

Piazza Adriana

Piazza
Cavour

Via Triboniano

Via Ulpiano

Lgt Prati

4

Largo di
Porta
Castello

Giardini di
Castel Sant'Angelo

Borgo Pio

Borgo Sant'Angelo

*Castel
Sant'Angelo*

Piazza Pia

Tourist
Information Point

👁 2

Lgt Castello

Ponte
Umberto I

Lgt Marzio

**Via della
Conciliazione**

Via San Pio X

3 ⊙ Ponte
Sant'Angelo

Tiber River

Piazza
Cavour

Piazza
Ponte
Umberto I

Via dell'Orso

Largo I
Gregore

Ponte Vittorio
Emanuele II

Lgt Tor di Nona

Via di Porta Santo Spirito

Lgt in Sassia

Lgt della Fiorentini

Corso Vittorio Emanuele II

Piazza
dell'Oro

Piazza di
San Salvatore
in Lauro

Via dei Coronari

Piazza
Lacellotti

Piazza
di Monte
Vecchio

Largo
Febo

5

Ponte
Principe
Amedeo

Sights

Piazza San Pietro
PIAZZA

1 Map p148, D4

Seen from above, 17th-century St Peter's Square resembles a giant keyhole with two semicircular colonnades encircling a giant ellipse that straightens out to funnel believers into St Peter's Basilica. The 25m obelisk was brought to Rome by Caligula from Egypt and later used by Nero as a turning post for chariot races. (MOttaviano-San Pietro)

Castel Sant'Angelo
CASTLE

2 Map p148, F4

Originally a mausoleum for Hadrian, this landmark castle was converted into a papal fortress in the 6th century. A secret passageway to the Vatican palaces was added in 1277, allowing Pope Clemente VII to escape here during the 1527 Sack of Rome. Its upper floors boast sumptuous Renaissance interiors, while the terrace (immortalised in Puccini's opera *Tosca*) offers aria-worthy views. (Lungotevere Castello 50; adult/reduced €8.50/6 plus possible exhibition supplement; ⊙9am-7.30pm Tue-Sun; 🚌Piazza Pia)

Ponte Sant'Angelo
BRIDGE

3 Map p148, F4

Opposite Castel Sant'Angelo, this bridge was built by Hadrian in AD 134 to provide an approach to his mausoleum. In the 17th century, Bernini and his pupils sculpted the figures of angels that line the pedestrian walkway. (🚌Piazza Pia)

Top Tip

Meet the Pope

At 11am on Wednesdays, the pope addresses his flock at the Vatican (in July and August in Castel Gandolfo, just outside of Rome). For details of how to apply for free tickets, see the **Vatican** (www.vatican.va/various/prefet tura/index_en.html) website.

The pope also blesses the crowd in Piazza San Pietro on Sunday at noon – no tickets are required.

Eating

Pizzarium
PIZZA AL TAGLIO €

4 Map p148, A3

A gourmet revelation masquerading as an unassuming takeaway, hard-to-find Pizzarium makes some of Rome's best sliced pizza. Served on a chopping board, its fluffy dough and perfect crust are topped with original, intensely flavoured ingredients. There's also a daily selection of *supplì* (crunchy rice croquettes), juices and chilled beers. (Via della Meloria 43; pizza slices from €3; ⊙11am-9pm Mon-Sat; MCipro-Musei Vaticani)

Gelarmony
GELATERIA €

5 Map p148, G2

A superb Sicilian gelateria, ideal for a lunchtime dessert, a mid-afternoon treat, an evening fancy – in fact, anything any time. Alongside 60 flavours of ice cream, there's a devilish selection of creamy sweets, including the best *cannoli* (pastry shells with a sweet filling of ricotta or custard) this side of Palermo. (Via Marcantonio Colonna 34; ice cream from €1.50; ⏰10am-late; Ⓜ Lepanto)

L'Arcangelo

GASTRONOMIC €€€

6 🍴 Map p148, G3

Local foodies are quick to recommend this elegant gem where politicians and celebs sit down to Roman classics such as tripe with mint and *pecorino* cheese, and more adventurous modern creations such as spicy pigeon with apples and mustard. The wine list also merits attention, with some interesting labels by small Italian producers. (✆06 321 09 92; Via Gioachino Belli 59-61; meals €60-70; ⏰lunch & dinner Mon-Fri, dinner Sat; Ⓜ Lepanto)

Hostaria Dino & Tony

TRATTORIA €€

7 🍴 Map p148, C2

While Tony stirs the pots, Dino delivers songs, punchlines and mammoth portions of simple Roman soul food. The *pasta alla grigia* (pasta with *pecorino* cheese, pancetta and black-pepper sauce) is legendary, while the heaving antipasto platter (think prosciutto, croquettes, rocket-laced pizza and vegetables au gratin) is a belt-busting feast. No credit cards. (✆06 3973 3284; Via Leone IV 60; meals €30-35; ⏰Mon-Sat; Ⓜ Ottaviano-San Pietro)

PAOLO CORDELLI/LONELY PLANET IMAGES ©

Del Frate (p152)

Del Frate

WINE BAR €€

8 Map p148, E2

Vino-versed locals love this wine shop with its simple wooden tables and brick-arched rooms. There's a formidable wine and cheese list and a small but refined menu of tartares, salads and fresh pastas. (☑06 323 64 37; www. enotecadelfrate.it; Via degli Scipioni 122; meals €40; ☺Mon-Sat; ⓜOttaviano-San Pietro)

Dolce Maniera

BAKERY €

9 Map p148, D1

Day or night, this buzzing basement bakery keeps the munchies at bay with its diet-defying snacks. Devour fresh *panini* (sandwiches), slabs of pizza, pastries, cakes and obscenely cheap *cornetti* (Italian croissants) in their every variation. (Via Barletta 27; ☺24hr; ⓜOttaviano-San Pietro)

Osteria dell'Angelo

TRATTORIA €€

10 Map p148, D1

Ex-rugby player Angelo presides over this hugely popular neighbourhood trattoria (reservations are a must). The set menu features a mixed antipasti, a robust Roman-style pasta and a choice of hearty mains with a side dish. To finish off, you're offered lightly spiced biscuits to dunk in sweet dessert wine. No credit cards. (☑06 372 94 70; Via Bettolo 24; set menu €25; ☺lunch & dinner Tue-Fri, dinner Mon & Sat; ⓜOttaviano-San Pietro)

Shanti

INDIAN €€

11 Map p148, E2

When you need a change from pizza and pasta, this dependable subcontinental restaurant dishes up delicately spiced dishes in a handsome, softly lit setting. Alongside tandooris, curries, dhals and naans, there are three set menus – vegetarian (€20), meat (€23) or fish (€26) – offering good value for money. (☑06 324 49 22; www.ristorante shanti.it; Via Fabio Massimo 68; meals €30; ⓜOttaviano-San Pietro)

Drinking

Art Studio Café

CAFE

12 Map p148, F2

A cafe, exhibition space and craft school all in one, this bright and breezy spot serves one of Prati's most popular aperitifs. It's also good for a light lunch – something like chicken couscous or fresh salad – or a restorative mid-afternoon tea. (www.artstudio cafe.it; Via dei Gracchi 187a; ☺Mon-Sat; ⓜOttaviano-San Pietro)

Passaguai

WINE BAR

13 Map p148, E3

A cave-like basement wine bar, Passaguai has a few outdoor tables and feels pleasingly off the beaten track. There's a good wine list and a range of artisanal beers, as well as tasty cheeses and cold cuts. (www.passaguai.it; Via Leto 1; ☺10am-2am Mon-Sat; ▯Piazza del Risorgimento)

Makasar   WINE BAR

14 Map p148, E4

Recharge your batteries with a quiet drink at this tranquil oasis. Choose from the nine-page tea menu or opt for wine and sit back with a book in the bottle-lined interior. (www.makasar.it; Via Plauto 33; ▣ Piazza del Risorgimento)

Entertainment

Alexanderplatz   LIVE MUSIC

15 ⭐ Map p148, C2

Small and intimate, Rome's top jazz club attracts sterling local and foreign acts (regulars include George Coleman and Lionel Hampton) and a respectful, cosmopolitan crowd. Book a table if you want to dine to the tunes. (✆ 06 3974 2171; www.alexanderplatz.it; Via Ostia 9; ⊙ concerts 9.45pm Sun-Thu, 10.30pm Sat & Sun; Ⓜ Ottaviano-San Pietro)

Fonclea   LIVE MUSIC

16 ⭐ Map p148, E3

A great little pub venue for live music, with bands playing anything from jazz to rockabilly, funk to African sounds (gigs start at 9.30pm). From June to August it moves to a riverside site under the Ponte Palatino on the Tiber. (www.fonclea.it; Via Crescenzio 82a; ⊙ 7pm-2am; ▣ Piazza del Risorgimento)

Shopping

C.U.C.I.N.A.   KITCHENWARE

17 🔒 Map p148, H3

If you're into cooking as much for the gear as the food, you'll enjoy this cool kitchenware shop. A branch of the capital's C.U.C.I.N.A. chain, it stocks all sorts of sexy pots and pans, designer cutlery, gourmet gadgets, wine glasses and a full range of dashing cooking fashions. (www.cucinastore.com; Via Gioachino Belli 21; ⊙ 10am-7.30pm Mon-Sat; ▣ Piazza Cavour)

Centro Russia Ecumenica Il Messaggio dell'Icona   SOUVENIRS

18 🔒 Map p148, D4

One person's holy icon is another's religious kitsch. Either way, the glittery collection of Byzantine-style icons and prayer cards make great original souvenirs, whether you're buying for God-fearing *nonna* or postmodern pals. (Borgo Pio 141; ⊙ 9am-7pm Mon-Sat, 10am-5pm Sun; ▣ Piazza del Risorgimento)

Outlet Gente   FASHION, ACCESSORIES

19 🔒 Map p148, E3

If your credit card doesn't cut it at the main Gente store (p64), try your luck in its basement outlet, where anything from Prada loafers to Miu Miu threads are subject to democratic markdowns of up to 50%. (Via Cola di Rienzo 246; ⊙ 3.30-7.30pm Mon & Sun, 10am-7.30pm Tue-Sat; Ⓜ Ottaviano-San Pietro)

Explore

Villa Borghese & Around

Villa Borghese, Rome's best-known park, is a lush, landscaped oasis of green. Once the grounds of a powerful 17th-century cardinal, it harbours some excellent galleries, including the superlative Museo e Galleria Borghese, and a superb Etruscan museum. To the east, in a smart residential district, MACRO – a former brewery turned modern art gallery – presents a more contemporary picture.

The Sights in a Day

Having reserved your ticket in advance, head to the **Museo e Galleria Borghese** (p156) to kick-start your day with a blast of Renaissance and baroque art. You're only allowed two hours in the museum but that's time enough to get the picture. Afterwards, take a stroll through **Villa Borghese** (p160), making sure to stop for a photo call on the Pincio before an early lunch at **Cinecaffè** (p162).

Walk off your lunch by heading down to the park's western flank, where you can choose between Italian impressionists at the **Galleria Nazionale d'Arte Moderna** (p160) or Etruscan sarcophagi at the **Museo Nazionale Etrusco di Villa Giulia** (p160). Alternatively, head east from Villa Borghese for a change of scene at contemporary art gallery **Museo d'Arte Contemporanea di Roma** (MACRO; p161).

Finish the day in style with a romantic dinner in the refined, neoclassical surroundings of the **Caffè delle Arti** (p162).

 Top Sights

Museo e Galleria Borghese (p156)

Best of Rome

Museums & Galleries

Museo e Galleria Borghese (p156)

Museo Nazionale Etrusco di Villa Giulia (p160)

Galleria Nazionale d'Arte Moderna (p160)

Culture

Auditorium Parco della Musica (p163)

Silvano Toti Globe Theatre (p163)

Casa del Cinema (p163)

For Free

Villa Borghese (p160)

Getting There

Ⓜ **Metro** To get to Villa Borghese follow the signs from Spagna (line A) or walk up from Flaminio (line A).

🚌 **Bus** Take bus 116, 52 or 53 to Villa Borghese from Via Vittorio Veneto near Barberini metro station.

🚊 **Tram** Tram 2 trundles up Via Flaminia from Piazzale Flaminio; tram 3 connects Piazza Thorvaldsen with Testaccio.

Top Sights
Museo e Galleria Borghese

If you only have the time, or inclination, for one art gallery in Rome, make it this one. Housing the 'queen of all private art collections', including works by Caravaggio, Bernini, Botticelli and Raphael, it provides the perfect introduction to Renaissance and baroque art without ever being overwhelming. To limit numbers, visitors are admitted at two-hourly intervals, so you'll need to call to prebook, and then enter at an allotted time. Trust us, though, it's worth it.

Map p158, E3

06 3 28 10

www.galleriaborghese.it

Piazzale del Museo Borghese

adult/reduced €9/4.50 plus €2 booking fee

9am-7pm Tue-Sun

Via Pinciana

Bernini's *Ratto di Proserpina*

Don't Miss

The Villa

Known as the Casino Borghese, the villa was built by Cardinal Scipione Borghese (1579–1633) to house his huge art collection. It was later given a neoclassical revamp and now has a ground-floor museum and upstairs picture gallery.

Venere Vincitrice

Antonio Canova's daring depiction of Napoleon's sister, Paolina Bonaparte Borghese, reclining top-less as *Venere Vincitrice* (Venus Victrix; 1805–08) dominates Sala 1. Apparently, Paolina had quite a reputation and when asked how she could have posed almost naked, she supposedly replied that it wasn't cold.

Ratto di Proserpina

Even in such hallowed company, Gian Lorenzo Bernini's spectacular sculptures – flamboyant depictions of pagan myths – steal the limelight. Just look at Pluto's hand pressing into the seem-ingly soft flesh of Persephone's thigh in the *Rape of Proserpina* (1621–22) or Daphne's hands mor-phing into leaves in *Apollo e Dafne* (1622–25).

Ragazzo col Canestro di Frutta

Caravaggio dominates Sala VIII. Here you can gaze on the *Boy with a Basket of Fruit* (1593–95), one of the artist's earliest and best-loved canvases. In its realism and use of chiaroscuro, it reveals the styles that were later to become Caravaggio trademarks.

Amor Sacro e Amor Profano

One of the museum's most important works, Titian's masterpiece *Sacred and Profane Love* (1514) depicts heavenly love (represented by a nude figure) and earthly love (a clothed figure).

☑ Top Tips

▶ You can reserve and pay for tickets online at www.tosc.it.

▶ If you have a Roma Pass (p196) you can only book by phone.

▶ Pick your ticket up from the ticket office 30 minutes before your entry time. Take ID.

▶ You only have two hours, which is enough, but keep track of the time.

✕ Take a Break

For a bite to eat there are several options in the surrounding Villa Borghese park. For something casual head to the Cinecaffè (p162), where you can pick up snacks, salads and a se-lection of pasta dishes. For a more stately venue, the Caffè delle Arti (p162) is a smart cafe offering coffee and full meals at the Gal-leria Nazionale d'Arte Moderna.

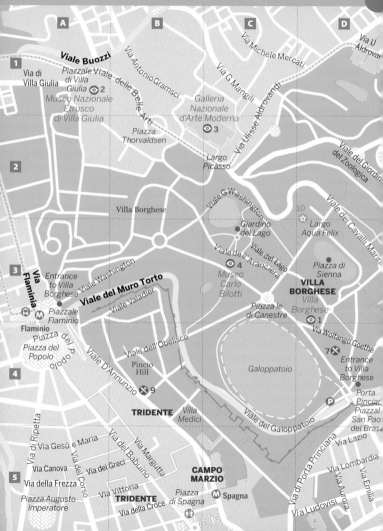

A
B
C
D

Viale Buozzi

Via di Villa Giulia

Piazzale di Villa Giulia ⊙ 2

Museo Nazionale Etrusco di Villa Giulia

Via Antonio Gramsci

Viale delle Belle Arti

Piazza Thorvaldsen

Via Michele Mercati

Via G Mangili

Galleria Nazionale d'Arte Moderna ⊙ 3

Via Ulisse Aldrovandi

Via U Aldrovar

Viale dei Giordini del Zoologica

Largo Picasso

Villa Borghese

Viale G Washington

Giardino del Lago

Largo Aqua Felix

10

Viale dei Cavalli Marini

Via Flaminia

Entrance to Villa Borghese

Viale Washington

Viale del Muro Torto

Viale Valadier

Viale dell'Aranciera

Museo Carlo Bilotti ⊙ 4

Viale del Lago

Piazza di Sienna

VILLA BORGHESE

Villa Borghese

Piazza le di Canestre

⊙ 1

Via Woltango Goethe

Piazzale Flaminio

Flaminio

Piazza del Popolo

Piazza del Popolo

Viale D'Annunzio

Viale dell'Obelisco

Pincio Hill

✕ 9

Villa Medici

Galoppatoio

7 ✕

Entrance to Villa Borghese

Porta Pinciar Piazzal San Pao del Bras

Via di Ripetta

Via Gesù e Maria

Via Canova

Via della Frezza

Via del Babuino

Via Margutta

Via dei Greci

Via Vittoria

Via della Croce

TRIDENTE

Piazza Augusto Imperatore

TRIDENTE

CAMPO MARZIO

Piazza di Spagna

Ⓜ Spagna

Viale del Galoppatoio

Via di Porta Princiana

Via Lazio

Via Lombardia

Via Aurora

Via Emilia

Via Ludovisi

400 m
0.2 miles

E Viale G Rossini
V G Carissimi
Via G Paisiello
Piazza G Verdi
F
Via S Mercadante
Viale Liegi
G
Via Salaria
Piazza Buenos Aires
Via Tirso
Via Tagliamento
Via Dora 6
Quartiere Coppedè
H
Via Tanaro
1

Largo N Spinelli
Via Metauro
Via Terso
Viale Regina Margherita
Via Ombrone

Piazza Giardino Zoologico
Via Po
Via Basento
2

Viale dei Pupozzi
Piazzale del Museo Borghese
Museo e Galleria Borghese
Via Tevere
Viale del Museo Borghese
Entrance to Villa Borghese
Via Po
Via di Villa Albani
Museo d'Arte Contemporanea di Roma (MACRO)
Via Nizza 5
3
Via Cagliari

Via Pinciana
Via G Puccini
Via Teresa
Via Savoia
Via Salaria
Via Veletri
8
SALARIO
Via Mantova
Via Reggio Emilia
Via Anieni
Piazza Fiume
Via Bergamo
Via Messina
Via Nomentana
4

Corso d'Italia
Via Campania
Via Romagna
Via Puglie
Via Calabria
Corso d'Italia
Porta Pia
Via Ancona
Piazza Porta Pia

Via Sardegna
Via Piemonte
Via Marche
Via Toscana
Via Abruzzi
Via Boncompagni

SALLUSTIANO
Via Sicilia
Via Lucullo
Via Sallustiana
Via Piave
Via Goito
Via Palestro
Via Cernaia
Via Montebello
5

Via Vittorio
Via Friuli

For reviews see	
◉ Top Sights	p156
◎ Sights	p160
✕ Eating	p162
✿ Entertainment	p163

Sights

Villa Borghese
PARK

1 Map p158, D3

Rome's Central Park, Villa Borghese is a top spot to catch your breath. Join the locals, lovers, tourists and joggers to stroll its landscaped lanes and explore landmarks such as the English-style Giardino del Lago and Piazza di Siena, an amphitheatre used to stage Rome's top equestrian event in May. Enjoy stunning views from Pincio hill or hire a bike for about €5 per hour. (entrances at Piazzale San Paolo del Brasile, Piazzale Flaminio & Via Pinciana; dawn-dusk; Porta Pinciana)

Museo Nazionale Etrusco di Villa Giulia
MUSEUM

2 Map p158, A1

Classicists will drool over Italy's finest collection of Etruscan booty, housed in Pope Julius III's 16th-century summer house. Among the prized possessions are the touchingly intimate 6th-century-BC Etruscan *Sarcofago degli sposi;* a polychrome terracotta statue of an armless *Apollo of Veio*; and the 2500-year-old *Euphronius Krater*, considered one of the world's finest examples of Hellenic pottery. (www .villagiulia.beniculturali.it; Piazzale di Villa Giulia 9; adult/reduced €8/4; 8.30am-7.30pm Tue-Sun; Viale delle Belle Arti)

Galleria Nazionale d'Arte Moderna
GALLERY

3 Map p158, C2

This oft-overlooked gallery of modern and contemporary art is one of Rome's coolest art museums. There are canvases by the *macchiaioli* (Italian Impressionists) and futurists, as well as impressive sculptures by Canova and major works by Modigliani and Giorgio de Chirico. International artists are also represented, with works by Degas, Cezanne, Kandinsky, Klimt, Mondrian, Pollock and Henry Moore. (www.gnam.beniculturali.it; Viale delle Belle Arti 131; adult/reduced €8/4; 8.30am-7.30pm Tue-Sun; Piazza Thorvaldsen)

Museo Carlo Bilotti
GALLERY

4 Map p158, C3

Drop into Villa Borghese's Orangery to eye up a small yet superb collection of art amassed by late Italo-American cosmetics tycoon Carlo Bilotti. Paintings range from a Warhol portrait of Bilotti's wife and late daughter, to 18 works by Italian great Giorgio de Chirico. Frequent temporary exhibitions are also staged. (www.museocarlobilotti.it;

Top Tip

Avoid Mondays

Monday is not a good day to explore Villa Borghese. Sure, you can walk the park, but all of the museums and galleries are shut – they open Tuesday to Sunday.

MARTIN MOOS/LONELY PLANET IMAGES ©

Renaissance loggia, Museo Nazionale Etrusco di Villa Giulia

Viale Fiorello La Guardia; adult/reduced €8/7; ⊘10am-4pm Tue-Fri Oct-May, 1-7pm Tue-Fri Jun-Sep, 10am-7pm Sat & Sun year-round; 🚊Porta Pinciana)

Museo d'Arte Contemporanea di Roma (MACRO)
GALLERY

5 ◉ Map p158, H3

Worth a visit as much for its architecture as art, MACRO wears a sophisticated steel-and-glass look courtesy of French architect Odile Decq's revamp of a former brewery. In the sexy black-and-red interior, exhibits include paintings, installations, video projections and sculptures by Italy's most important post-WWII artists. (www.macro.roma.museum; adult/reduced €11.50/9.50; Via Nizza 138, cnr Via Cagliari; ⊘11am-7pm Tue-Fri & Sun, to 10pm Sat; 🚊Via Nizza)

Quartiere Coppedè
NEIGHBOURHOOD

6 ◉ Map p158, H1

Best entered from the corner of Via Tagliamento and Via Dora, this compact quarter is a mesmerising mishmash of Tuscan turrets, Liberty sculptures, Moorish arches, Gothic gargoyles, frescoed facades and palm-fringed gardens – all designed by little-known Florentine architect Gino Coppedè in the 1920s. Look out for the charming Fontana delle Rane (Fountain of the Frogs). (🚊🚊Viale Regina Margherita)

Eating

Cinecaffè
CAFE €€

7 Map p158, D4

Part of the Casa del Cinema complex (p163), this slick, modern cafe is one of the few places to get a decent bite in Villa Borghese. Stop by for a quick coffee or claim a table on the sunny terrace for an alfresco salad or choice pasta. Snacks and panini are also available and brunch is served at weekends. (www.cinecaffe.it; Casina delle Rose, Largo Marcello Mastroianni 1; snacks from €2.50, salads €9; ⊙9am-7pm; 🚇Porta Pinciana)

Caffè delle Arti
CAFE €€

The cafe-cum-restaurant of the Galleria Nazionale d'Arte Moderna (see 3 ◉ Map p158, C2), the Caffè delle Arti sits in glorious neoclassical splendour in a leafy corner of Villa Borghese. A refined spot, it's at its best on sultry summer nights, when you can sit on the terrace and revel in the romantic atmosphere over coffee, cocktails or a full à la carte dinner. (☎06 3265 1236; Via Gramsci 73; meals €45; ⊙7.45am-12.30am Tue-Sun, to 6pm Mon; 🚇🚌Piazza Thorvaldsen)

Serenella
PIZZA AL TAGLIO €

8 Map p158, G3

It's a bit out of the way, unless you're walking from Villa Borghese to MACRO, but this innocuous-looking pizza takeaway is a top pit-stop. It claims to use natural yeast in its pizza bases, which might or might not explain why the pizza *bianca* (a topping-free

---

Understand
Football-Crazy Rome

Forget St Peter's Basilica. Rome's true centre of worship is the Stadio Olimpico, the city's hallowed football stadium where Rome's two Serie A (premier league) sides play during the season from late August to May.

Footballing passions run high in *calcio*-crazy Rome, with fans' loyalties divided between AS Roma (*i giallorossi* – the yellow and reds) and their bitter rivals SS Lazio (*i biancazzuri* – the white and blues). Since the heady days of 2000, when Lazio won the title, and 2001, when Roma claimed the honours, both sides have been beset by financial problems and have reverted back to being solid, mid-table performers.

Lazio's *tifosi* (fans) traditionally come from the provincial towns outside Rome, while Roma's supporters, known as *romanisti*, are historically working class, from Rome's Jewish community and from Trastevere, Testaccio and Garbatella.

white pizza) is so good – light, crispy and delicately salted. (Via Salaria 70; pizza slices from €1.50; ⏱9am-7pm; 🚌Via Pinciana)

Casina Valadier   MEDITERRANEAN €€€

9 Map p158, B4

Housed in a neoclassical lodge, this palatial restaurant is perfect for a romantic rendezvous with its sophisticated food, citrus-sprinkled garden and panoramic views. (📞06 699 22 090; www.casinavaladier.it; Piazza Bucarest; meals from €70; ⏱Mon-Sat; Ⓜ Flaminio)

Entertainment

Casa del Cinema   CINEMA

In Villa Borghese, the Casa del Cinema comprises an exhibition space, three projection halls and a popular cafe (see 7 Map p158, D4). It screens everything from documentaries to shorts, indie flicks and arthouse classics (sometimes in their original language) and hosts a regular program of film-related events and book presentations. (📞06 06 08; www.casadelcinema.it; Largo Marcello Mastroianni 1; 🚌Porta Pinciana)

Silvano Toti Globe Theatre   THEATRE

10 ⭐ Map p158, D2

Like London's Globe Theatre, but with better weather, this open-air Elizabethan theatre in the middle of Villa Borghese serves up Shakespeare (mostly in Italian but with the occasional performance in English) from July to September. Scan the website for upcoming shows and box-office times. Tickets start at €10 for a place in the stalls, rising up to €23. (📞06 06 08; www.globetheatreroma.com; Largo Aqua Felix; 🚌Piazzale Brasile)

The Best of
Rome

Spanish Steps (p56) and Chiesa della Trinità dei Monti (p57)
GEOFF STRINGER/LONELY PLANET IMAGES ©

Best Walks
Emperors' Footsteps

🏃 The Walk

Follow in the footsteps of Rome's legendary emperors on this walk around the best of the city's ancient treasures. Established in 27 BC, the Roman Empire grew to become the Western world's first dominant superpower and at the peak of its power, in about AD 100, it extended from Britain to north Africa, and from Syria to Spain. Rome itself had a population of more than 1.5 million and all of the trappings of imperial splendour: marble temples, public baths, theatres, shopping centres and, of course, the Colosseum.

Start Colosseum; **M** Colosseo

Finish Il Vittoriano; 🚌 Piazza Venezia

Length 1.5km; all morning (moving fast)

🍴 Take a Break

Hidden away in the Capitoline Museums but accessible by its own entrance, the Caffè Capitolino (p35) is a refined spot for a restorative coffee.

Capitoline Museums (p31)

❶ Colosseum

More than any other monument, it's the **Colosseum** (p24) that symbolises the power and glory of ancient Rome. A spectacular feat of engineering, the 50,000-seat stadium was inaugurated by Emperor Titus in AD 80 with a bloodthirsty bout of games that lasted 100 days and nights.

❷ Palatino

A short walk from the Colosseum, past the **Arco di Costantino**, the **Palatino** (p31) was ancient Rome's most sought-after neighbourhood, home to the emperor and cream of imperial society. The evocative ruins are confusing but their scale gives some sense of the luxury in which the ancient VIPs liked to live.

❸ Roman Forum

Coming down from the Palatino you'll enter the **Roman Forum** (p26) near the **Arco di Tito**, one of Rome's great triumphal arches. In imperial times, the forum was the empire's nerve centre, a teeming hive of law courts, temples, piazzas and shops. The vestal virgins lived here and senators debated matters of state in the **Curia**.

④ Piazza del Campidoglio

Considered by many to be Rome's most beautiful square, the Michelangelo-designed **Piazza del Campidoglio** (p31) sits atop the Campidoglio (Capitoline hill), one of the seven hills on which Rome was founded. In ancient times this was the spiritual heart of the

city, home to two of the city's most important temples: one dedicated to Jupiter Capitolinus, and the other to Juno Moneta.

⑤ Capitoline Museums

Occupying two stately *palazzi* (mansions) on Piazza del Campidoglio, the **Capitoline Museums** (p31), the world's oldest public museums, house a superb collection of classical Roman sculpture. But before starting on the collections proper, check out the masonry littered

around the ground-floor courtyard. Most of it comes from a 12m-high statue of Emperor Constantine, which originally stood in the Roman Forum.

⑥ Il Vittoriano

From the Campidoglio, pop next door to the massive mountain of white marble that is **Il Vittoriano** (p31). No emperor ever walked here, but it's worth stopping off to take the panoramic lift to the top, from where you can see the whole of Rome laid out beneath you.

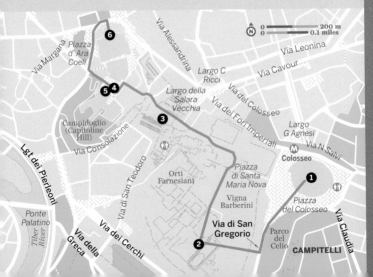

Best Walks
Piazzas of Rome

🏃 The Walk

Rome's tightly packed historic centre boasts some of the city's most celebrated piazzas, and several beautiful but lesser known squares. Each has its own character – the baroque splendour of Piazza Navona, the bawdy clamour of Campo de' Fiori, the Renaissance elegance of Piazza Farnese – but together they encapsulate much of the city's beauty, history and drama. Take this tour to discover the best of them and enjoy the area's vibrant street life.

Start Largo di Torre Argentina; 🚌🚊Largo di Torre Argentina

Finish Piazza Farnese; 🚌Corso Vittorio Emanuele II

Length 1.5km; two to three hours

🍴 Take a Break

Between the Pantheon and Piazza Navona, the Caffè Sant'Eustachio (p50) is a good bet for a quick pit stop. Its coffee is reckoned by many to be the best in the capital.

Flower stall in Campo de' Fiori (p47)

❶ Largo di Torre Argentina

Start off in **Largo di Torre Argentina**, set around the sunken ruins of four Republic-era temples. On the piazza's western flank, the **Teatro Argentina** (p52) sits near the site where Julius Caesar was assassinated.

❷ Piazza della Minerva

Head along Via dei Cestari until you come to Piazza della Minerva and the **Elefantino** (p45), a sculpture of a puzzled elephant carrying an Egyptian obelisk. Flanking the square, the Gothic **Chiesa di Santa Maria Sopra Minerva** boasts Renaissance frescoes and a minor Michelangelo.

❸ Piazza di Sant'Ignazio Loyola

Strike off down Via Santa Caterina da Siena, then take Via del Piè di Marmo and Via di Sant'Ignazio to reach the exquisite 18th-century **Piazza di Sant'Ignazio Loyola** (p45). Overlooking the piazza, the **Chiesa di Sant'Ignazio di Loyola** features a magical trompe l'œil ceiling fresco.

❹ Piazza della Rotonda

A short stroll down Via del Seminario brings you to the bustling, cafe-filled **Piazza della Rotonda**, where the **Pantheon** (p38) needs no introduction. Rome's best-preserved ancient building is one of the city's iconic sights with its epic portico and record-breaking dome.

❺ Piazza Navona

From the Pantheon, follow the signs to **Piazza Navona** (p44), central Rome's great showpiece square. Here, among the street artists, tourists and pigeons, you can compare the two giants of Roman baroque (see p73) – Gian Lorenzo Bernini, creator of the **Fontana dei Quattro Fiumi**, and Francesco Borromini, author of the **Chiesa di Sant'Agnese in Agone**.

❻ Campo de' Fiori

On the other side of Corso Vittorio Emanuele II, the busy road that bisects the *centro storico* (historic centre), life is focused on **Campo de' Fiori** (p47). By day, this noisy square stages a colourful market, but at night it transforms into a raucous open-air pub.

❼ Piazza Farnese

Just beyond the Campo, **Piazza Farnese** is a re-fined square overlooked by the Renaissance **Palazzo Farnese** (p47). This magnificent *palazzo*, now home to the French embassy, boasts some superb frescoes, said by some to rival those of the Sistine Chapel.

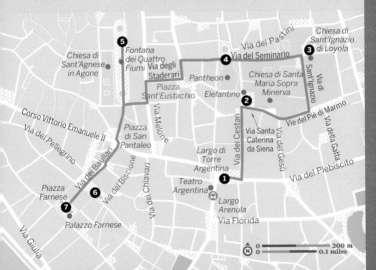

Best
History

For thousands of years Rome was at the centre of world events. First, as *caput mundi* (capital of the world), the glittering hub of the vast Roman Empire, and then as the seat of papal power. It was a city that counted and this is writ large on its historic streets, where every *palazzo*, church and ancient ruin has a tale to tell.

RUSSELL MOUNTFORD/LONELY PLANET IMAGES ©

Ancient Glories

Many of Rome's most thrilling monuments hark back to its golden age as capital of the mighty Roman Empire. The Colosseum, the Pantheon, the Roman Forum – these epic ruins all tell of past glories in a way that no textbook ever can, evoking images of teeming crowds and gladiatorial combat, pagan ceremonies and daily drama.

The Church Rules

For much of its history, the Church called the shots in Rome and many of the city's top sights are religious in origin. Early basilicas stand testament to the tenacity of the Church's founding fathers, while the masterpieces that litter the city's churches testify to the wealth and ambition of the Renaissance and baroque popes.

Multilayered History

One of Rome's characteristic features is the way that history quite literally rises from the ground. Over the centuries the city has undergone several transformations and with each one a new layer was added to the city's urban fabric. As a result, medieval churches stand over pagan temples and baroque piazzas carpet Roman circuses. In Rome, to travel back in time you merely have to go underground.

Best Roman Relics

Colosseum (p24) Rome's iconic arena embodies all the drama of the ancient city.

Pantheon (p38) This awe-inspiring building has served as an architectural blueprint for millennia.

Roman Forum (p26) The inspiring ruins of ancient Rome's bustling city centre.

Palatino (p31) Ancient emperors languished in luxury on the Palatino, imperial Rome's oldest and most exclusive neighbourhood.

Terme di Caracalla (p111) The towering remains of this ancient leisure centre are among Rome's most impressive.

Best for Going Underground

Basilica di San Clemente (p99)
This medieval basilica sits over a pagan temple and 1st-century house.

Catacombs (p106) The Appian Way (Via Appia Antica) is riddled with catacombs where the early Christians buried their dead.

Chiesa di SS Giovanni e Paolo & Case Romane (p99) Head underground to the Case Romane to explore the houses where apostles John and Paul supposedly once lived.

Museo Nazionale Romano: Crypta Balbi (p47) A museum atop Renaissance ruins atop a 1st-century-BC theatre.

Best Historical Churches

St Peter's Basilica (p138) The Vatican's showpiece church stands over St Peter's tomb.

Basilica di San Giovanni in Laterano (pictured left; p96) The main papal basilica until the 14th century.

Basilica di San Paolo Fuori-le-Mura (p119) Monumental basilica on the site where St Paul was buried.

Chiesa del Gesù (p44) Important Jesuit church, home to Ignatius Loyola for 12 years.

Best for Legends

Palatino (p31) Where the wolf saved Romulus and Remus, and Rome was founded in 753 BC.

Bocca della Verità (p33) Tell a lie and the 'Mouth of Truth' will bite your hand off.

Basilica di San Pietro in Vincoli (p84) Houses the miraculous chains that bound St Peter.

Trevi Fountain (p68) Throw a coin in and you'll return to Rome.

Teatro Argentina (p52) Rome's top theatre stands near the site where Julius Caesar was assassinated.

Worth a Trip

Rome's answer to Pompeii, the **Scavi Archeologici di Ostia Antica** (Ruins of Ostia Antica; www.ostiaantica.net; Viale dei Romagnoli 717; adult/reduced €8/4; ⏲8.30am-7pm Tue-Sun Apr-Oct, to 6.30pm Oct, to 4.30pm Nov-Feb, to 5pm Mar) offer a well-preserved insight into ancient Rome's once-thriving port. Highlights include the Terme di Nettuno and the impressive amphitheatre. To get to the site take the suburban train from Piramide.

Best
Food

Food is central to the Roman passion for life. Everyone has an opinion on it and the city teems with trattorias, pizzerias, fine-dining restaurants and gourmet gelaterie. Traditional Roman cooking holds sway but *cucina creativa* (creative cooking) has taken off in recent years and there are plenty of exciting, contemporary restaurants to try.

RICHARD I'ANSON/LONELY PLANET IMAGES ©

The Traditional Trattoria

The bedrock of the Roman food scene has always been the family-run trattorias that pepper the city's streets and piazzas. These simple eateries, often with rickety wooden tables and *nonna* (grandma) at the stove, have been feeding visitors for centuries and are still the best bet for hearty, no-nonsense Roman dishes such as *bucatini all'amatriciana* (thick spaghetti with tomato sauce and *guanciale* – cured pig's cheek) and *spaghetti alla gricia* (with *pecorino* and pancetta).

Contemporary Fine Dining

Recently, a raft of new-wave trattorias and chic designer restaurants have opened, offering edgy, innovative food. Leading the way, Francesco Apreda of Imàgo (p60) and Cristina Bowerman of Glass Hostaria (p130) have made their names with modern, imaginative Italo-fusion fare.

Gourmet Takeaways

In Rome, the simplest snack can turn into a revelation thanks to a new breed of gourmet takeaways – *pizza al taglio* places offer sliced pizza topped with seasonal, high-quality ingredients, while gelaterie spoon out classic combos alongside exotic flavours made from delicacies such as Himalayan salt and pungent gorgonzola.

☑ **Top Tips**

▶ When you sit down in a trattoria or restaurant, you'll get a bread basket and be charged for it whether you eat it or not. This is standard practice, not a tourist rip-off.

▶ If you want bottled water, ask for *acqua naturale* (still) or *acqua frizzante* (sparkling).

▶ Round the bill up in a pizzeria in lieu of a tip; leave up to 10% in a more upmarket place.

Best Fine Dining

Glass Hostaria (p130) Designer Trastevere restaurant serving contemporary Italian food with an oriental twist.

Agata e Romeo (p87) Traditional Roman staples get a modern twist at this fine-dining stalwart.

La Rosetta (p48) Sit down to sumptuous seafood at this classy fish restaurant near the Pantheon.

Imàgo (p60) Haute cuisine and haute views from the rooftop restaurant of the five-star Hassler Hotel.

L'Arcangelo (p151) Dine on Roman classics and innovative fare at this Prati favourite.

Best Traditional

Flavio al Velavevodetto (p112) A relaxed, popular Testaccio trattoria serving excellent Roman and Italian classics.

Trattoria Monti (p86) Highly regarded restaurant specialising in earthy food from the region of Le Marche.

Armando al Pantheon (p47) A bastion of traditional Roman cuisine in the touristy Pantheon area.

Colline Emiliane (p75) An outpost of Emilia-Romagna celebrated for its handmade pastas and rich meat sauces.

Best Pizza al Taglio

Pizzarium (p150) Near the Vatican Museums, this is the best pizza takeaway in town.

Forno Roscioli (p48) A seriously good bakery-cum-deli in the historic centre.

Forno di Campo de' Fiori (p48) Always-busy bakery famous for its *pizza bianca* (white pizza).

00100 Pizza (p113) This blink-and-you'll-miss-it place flies the flag for gourmet pizza in Testaccio.

Da Michele (p75) The perfect spot for a sightseeing pit stop near the Trevi Fountain.

Best Ice Cream

Il Gelato di San Crispino (p75) When only the best will do. Famed for its natural, seasonal flavours.

Il Gelato (p114) Taste the experimental ice creams of Claudio Torcè, Rome's gelato king.

Grom (p49) The *centro storico* branch of Italy's much-vaunted gelato chain.

Palazzo del Freddo di Giovanni Fassi (p87) Grab a granita at this old-fashioned gem of a gelateria.

Gelarmony (p150) As well as delicious ice cream, it does a fab line in sticky Sicilian *dolci* (sweets).

Best
For Free

Although Rome is an expensive city, you don't have to break the bank to enjoy it. A surprising number of its big sights are free, including all churches, and it costs nothing to stroll the historic streets, piazzas and parks, basking in their extraordinary beauty. Free events are often staged during festivals and public holidays. Also check for initiatives offering free admission to museums and monuments.

W/BOWD RUSU/LONELY PLANET IMAGES ©

Best Places for Free Art

St Peter's Basilica (p138) Michelangelo's *Pietà* is just one of the masterpieces on display.

Basilica di San Pietro in Vincoli (p84) Feast your eyes on Michelangelo's fearsome *Moses*.

Chiesa di San Luigi dei Francesi (p44) Caravaggio's St Matthew cycle is the big drawcard here.

Chiesa di Santa Maria del Popolo (p59) Caravaggio, Raphael and Bernini all had a hand in this Renaissance church.

Chiesa di Santa Maria Sopra Minerva (p45) Rome's only Gothic church boasts its own Michelangelo sculpture.

Vatican Museums (p142) Free on the last Sunday of each month.

Best Piazzas & Parks

Piazza Navona (p44) A colourful cast of street artists adds to the atmosphere on this stunning baroque piazza.

Campo de' Fiori (p47) Revel in the cheerful chaos of the Campo's daily market.

Piazza del Popolo (p59) Sit under the central obelisk and watch the world go by.

Villa Borghese (p160) Rome's most celebrated park is ideal for leisurely strolling and lunchtime picnics.

Gianicolo (p124) Admire magnificent views from this leafy hill.

Best Free Monuments

Pantheon (p38) It doesn't cost a penny to enter this extraordinary church.

Trevi Fountain (p68) Throw a coin in to ensure your return to Rome.

Bocca della Verità (p33) Test the legend – tell a lie with your hand in the mouth.

Spanish Steps (p56) Grab a perch and hang out on Rome's most celebrated staircase.

Best
Bars & Nightlife

Nightlife in Rome is all about enjoying the vibe and lapping up the spectacular surroundings. The city's central streets buzz well into the night as locals crowd into popular bars and cafes before heading off late to a club. Clubbing action caters to most tastes, with DJs spinning everything from lounge and jazz to house, dancehall and hip hop.

KRZYSZTOF DYDYNSKI/LONELY PLANET IMAGES ©

Best Areas

Centro Storico (p52) Bars and a few clubs, a mix of touristy and sophisticated.

Trastevere (p133) Everyone's favourite evening hang-out, with plenty of bars and cafes.

Testaccio (p115) With a cluster of mainstream clubs, there's something for almost every taste.

Ostiense (p118) Home to Rome's cooler nightclubs, mostly housed in ex-industrial venues.

San Lorenzo & Il Pigneto (p92) Favoured by students and bohemians, with a concentration of bars and alternative clubs.

Best Bars & Cafes

Ai Tre Scalini (p88) Buzzing Monti wine bar with a pub-like vibe.

Caffè Sant'Eustachio (p50) Unglamorous cafe that serves the capital's best coffee.

Necci (p93) A historic Pigneto hang-out, once a favourite of film director Pier Paolo Pasolini.

Salotto 42 (p51) *Molto* trendy lounge bar on a picturesque piazza.

Best Clubs

Circolo degli Artisti (p93) Hosts top DJs and alternative-music gigs and has a cool beer garden.

☑ Top Tips

▶ Take your cue from the locals and dress up to go out, particularly in the *centro storico* and Testaccio.

▶ Some popular nightclubs have a seemingly whimsical door policy, and men, single or in groups, are often turned away.

Rashomon (p119) Dance your arse off to a mix of electro-rock, indie, reggae, hip hop and dancehall.

Conte Staccio (p115) One of the best venues on the mainstream Testaccio clubbing strip.

Best
Architecture

Boasting ancient ruins, Renaissance basilicas, baroque churches and hulking fascist *palazzi*, Rome's architectural legacy is unparalleled. Michelangelo, Bramante, Borromini and Bernini are among the architects who have stamped their genius on the remarkable cityscape, while in recent years a number of the world's top architects have completed projects in the city.

Ancient Engineering

In building their great capital, ancient Roman architects and engineers were called on to design houses, roads, aqueducts and shopping centres alongside temples, tombs and imperial palaces. To do so they advanced methods devised by the Etruscans and Greeks and developed construction techniques that allowed them to build on a hitherto unseen scale.

Renaissance & Baroque Makeovers

Many of Rome's great *palazzi* and basilicas date to the Renaissance 16th century, including St Peter's Basilica, which was given a complete overhaul by Bramante, Michelangelo et al. A century later, the Counter-Reformation paved the way for a Church-sponsored makeover led by the baroque heroes Gian Lorenzo Bernini and Francesco Borromini.

Modern Architecture

In the early 20th century, Italy's Fascist dictator Benito Mussolini oversaw a number of grandiose building projects, including Via dei Fori Imperiali and the EUR district. More recently, projects have been completed by Renzo Piano, Massimiliano Fuksas, Richard Meier and Zaha Hadid.

Best Ancient Monuments

Colosseum (p24) A blueprint for modern stadiums, it dramatically illustrates the use of the arch.

Pantheon (p38) The ancient Romans' greatest architectural achievement was revolutionary in both design and execution.

Terme di Caracalla (p111) These looming ruins hint at the sophistication of ancient building techniques.

Mercati di Traiano Museo dei Fori Imperiali (p32) A towering model of 2nd-century civic engineering.

Best Basilica Designs

Basilica di San Giovanni in Laterano (p96) Its original design was the blueprint for basilicas to follow.

Basilica di Santa Maria Maggiore (p84) The only one of Rome's four patriarchal basilicas to retain its original layout.

Basilica di Santa Sabina (p111) This medieval gem sports an austere, no-frills basilica look.

Best Renaissance Buildings

Tempietto del Bramante (p128) Bramante's influential masterpiece of harmonious design encapsulates High Renaissance ideals.

St Peter's Basilica (p138) An amalgamation of designs, styles and plans, capped by Michelangelo's extraordinary dome.

Palazzo Farnese (p47) Home to the French embassy, this is a fine example of a classical Renaissance palace.

Piazza del Campidoglio (p31) Michelangelo's hilltop piazza is a show-stopping model of Renaissance town planning.

Best Baroque Gems

Piazza San Pietro (p150) Bernini designed the Vatican's focal square to funnel believers into St Peter's Basilica.

Piazza Navona (p44) With a Borromini church and a Bernini fountain, this celebrated square

is a model of baroque beauty.

Chiesa di San Carlo alle Quattro Fontane (p72) Borromini's petite church bears many of his trademark tricks.

Best Modern Icons

Palazzo della Civiltà del Lavoro Known as the Square Colosseum, this *palazzo* is typical of 1930s rationalism.

Auditorium Parco della Musica (p163) Renzo Piano's avant-garde concert complex features a unique architectural design.

Museo dell'Ara Pacis (p59) Controversially designed by Richard Meier, this white pavilion houses an important 1st-century-BC altar.

Worth a Trip

One of the few planned developments in Rome's history, **EUR** was built for an international exhibition in 1942, the Esposizione Universale di Roma (Roman Universal Exhibition; EUR). There are a few museums, but the area's interest lies in its spectacular rationalist architecture – best expressed in the iconic **Palazzo della Civiltà del Lavoro** (Quadrato della Concordia; M EUR Magliana).

Best
Museums

WIBOWO RUSLI/LONELY PLANET IMAGES ©

Rome's museums and galleries pack quite a punch. Housed in frescoed *palazzi*, noble villas and ancient ruins, they showcase the city's price-less collection of ancient art, Renaissance treas-ures, baroque sculptures and futuristic paintings. The onus is on heavyweight art, but know where to go and you'll find there's more to Rome's mu-seums than Michelangelo and Caravaggio.

☑ Top Tips

▶ Most museums are closed on Mondays.

▶ EU citizens over 65 and under 18 often qualify for free admission. Take ID as proof of age.

▶ Many museums close their ticket offices up to 75 minutes before closing time.

Historic Collections

Throughout history, Rome's leaders have proved to be indefatigable collectors. None more so than the Catholic Church, whose vast collection is on display at the Vatican Museums (p142). An artistic goldmine, it includes everything from Egyptian mummies and Etruscan tombs to Old Masters and Michelangelo frescoes.

During the 16th and 17th centuries, the Church was the key sponsor of the arts and many of its senior officers were serious patrons. The most cele-brated was Cardinal Scipione Borghese, who put together the 'queen of all private art collections' for his personal residence – now the Museo e Gal-leria Borghese (p156). Cardinal Ludovico Ludovisi was another churchman with an eye for artistic genius, stockpiling much of the ancient sculpture that graces the Museo Nazionale Romano: Palazzo Altemps (p44).

Not Just Art

Despite appearances, Rome's museums are not all about ancient sculptures and Renaissance paint-ings. You can, for example, peruse poetic mem-orabilia in the house where John Keats penned his last words, or learn about the city's Jewish community in Rome's towering synagogue.

Best of the Best

Vatican Museums (p142) The Sistine Chapel and Raphael Rooms headline at this spectacular museum complex.

Museo e Galleria Borghese (p156) Houses Rome's best baroque sculpture and some superlative Old Masters.

Capitoline Museums (p31) Ancient sculpture is the main draw at the world's oldest public museums.

Museo Nazionale Romano: Palazzo Massimo alle Terme (p80) An overlooked gem boasting fabulous Roman sculpture and mosaics.

Museo Nazionale Romano: Palazzo Altemps (p44) Blazing baroque frescoes provide the background for classical sculpture.

Best Galleries

Galleria Doria Pamphilj (p44) A lavish gallery full of major works by big-name artists.

Galleria Nazionale d'Arte Antica – Palazzo Barberini (p71) A sumptuous baroque *palazzo* with paintings by Caravaggio, Raphael, Holbein et al.

Galleria Nazionale d'Arte Antica di Palazzo Corsini (p129) Part of Italy's national collection is displayed in this 16th-century palace.

Galleria Nazionale d'Arte Moderna (p160) Showcases modern works by important Italian and international artists.

Palazzo e Galleria Colonna (p71) Loud frescoes and bombastic paintings decorate the Colonna family's private gallery.

Best Museum Settings

Castel Sant'Angelo (p150) Admire lavish Renaissance interiors in this brooding, landmark castle.

Museo Nazionale Romano: Terme di Diocleziano (p84) Ancient Rome's largest baths complex provides a memorable backdrop for historic artefacts.

Mercati di Traiano Museo dei Fori Imperiali (p32) A museum set in Trajan's towering 2nd-century shopping mall.

Centrale Montemartini (p119) A former power station juxtaposes ancient sculpture with industrial machinery.

Museo dell'Ara Pacis (p59) An ancient altar is ensconced in a controversial modern pavilion.

Best Specialist Museums

Museo Nazionale Etrusco di Villa Giulia (p160) Italy's premier Etruscan museum.

Museo Ebraico di Roma (p48) Chronicles the turbulent past of Rome's long-standing Jewish community.

Keats-Shelley House (p59) Pay homage to Romantic poet Keats in the house where he died.

Museo Nazionale d'Arte Orientale (p85) Feast on oriental art at this little-known charmer.

Best
Shopping

Rome boasts the usual cast of flagship chain stores and glitzy designer outlets, but what makes it so special is its legion of small, independent shops – historic, family-owned delis, picture-framers, dusty furniture workshops, small-label fashion boutiques and artists studios. Adding to the fun are the much-frequented neighbourhood markets selling everything from second-hand jeans to bumper produce from local farms.

JEAN-PIERRE LESCOURRET/LONELY PLANET IMAGES ©

☑ Top Tips

▶ Many shops are closed on Monday morning.

▶ Make sure you take the receipt when you buy something.

▶ Tax rebates are available to non-EU residents who spend more than €155 in shops displaying a Tax Free sticker.

Shopping Areas

For designer clothes head to Via dei Condotti (Map p58, C4) and the area around Piazza di Spagna. You'll find vintage shops and fashion boutiques on Via del Governo Vecchio (Map p42, A4) in the *centro storico*, and in the Monti district. Testaccio is a good bet for foodie purchases, with one of Rome's best delis and a vibrant morning market.

Artisans

Rome has a surprising number of designers and artisans, who create and sell their goods in small, old-fashioned workshops. There are places you can get a bag, wallet or belt made to your specifications or order a tailored tie or dress. You'll find a number of these shops in the *centro storico*, Tridente and Monti areas.

Sales

Winter sales *(saldi)* run from early January to mid-February, and summer sales from July to early September.

Best Fashion

Abito (p90) Chic female fashions at this cool Monti boutique.

Eleonora (p64) Popular with fashionistas in the upmarket Tridente shopping district.

Arsenale (p52) Artistic clothes at the atelier of local designer Patrizia Pieroni.

Bomba (p64) A discreet showcase for high-quality knitwear and modish accessories.

Gente (p64) Big-name fashion brands at this glitzy department store.

Best Shoes & Accessories

Borini (p52) Locals head to this low-key shop for the latest shoes.

Fausto Santini (p64) A boutique with designer footwear and eye-catching bags.

La Cravatta su Misura (p134) Bespoke ties for the well-groomed modern gentleman.

Fabriano (p64) For stylish stationery and accessories – notebooks to smartphone sleeves and jewellery.

Furla (p65) Colourful bags, sunglasses and wallets all bear the popular Furla name.

Best Food & Wine

Volpetti (p116) Foodies rate this lavish deli as one of the best in town.

Confetteria Moriondo & Gariglio (p52) A historic chocolate shop straight out of central casting.

Antica Caciara Trastevere (p134) A Trastevere deli celebrated for its fab fresh cheeses.

Best Markets

Porta Portese (p135) Rome's historic Sunday-morning flea market on the banks of the Tiber.

Nuovo Mercato di Testaccio (p117) Noisy and colourful, Testaccio's market is a much-loved local institution.

Best Art

Home to some of the Western world's greatest art, Rome is a visual feast. Its churches contain more masterpieces than many midsize countries and its galleries are laden with instantly recognisable works. The city has starred in all major upheavals in Western art and the results are there for all to see – classical statues, stunning Renaissance frescoes and breathtaking baroque decor.

Ancient Sculpture & Mosaics

Early Roman sculpture focused on the human form, but later became more propagandistic, culminating in the use of commemorative reliefs. Mosaics were also popular, initially as decoration for private villas and later adorning churches.

The Renaissance

The Renaissance unleashed an artistic maelstrom as artists such as Michelangelo and Raphael set about decorating the city's basilicas, churches and palaces. Fresco painting was a key endeavour and many celebrated frescoes date to this period.

The Baroque

The baroque burst onto Rome's art scene in the early 17th century and was enthusiastically adopted by the Church as a propaganda tool in its battle against Reformation heresy. In artistic terms, the two leading lights were Gian Lorenzo Bernini and the controversial painter Caravaggio.

Modern Art

The 20th century saw the emergence of futurism, a nationalistic modernist movement; and metaphysical painting, an Italian form of surrealism best expressed in the works of Giorgio de Chirico.

Best Ancient Sculpture

Museo Pio-Clementino (p145) *Laocoön* and *Apollo belvedere* are the stars of this Vatican Museum.

Museo dell'Ara Pacis (p59) The Ara Pacis Augustae is a vast marble altar decorated with detailed reliefs of Augustus and family.

Capitoline Museums (p31) Check out the iconic *Lupa capitolina*, complete with babies Romulus and Remus, and the profoundly touching *Galata morente*.

Best Mosaics

Museo Nazionale Romano: Palazzo Massimo alle Terme (p80) Has some superb mosaics stripped from ancient villas.

Chiesa di Santa Prassede (p84) The best place to see golden Byzantine-style mosaics in situ.

Basilica di Santa Maria in Trastevere (p122) Famous for its 12th-century apse mosaics.

Basilica di Santa Maria Maggiore (p84) Boasts some wonderful 5th-century mosaics.

Best Renaissance Masterpieces

Sistine Chapel (p143) Home to Michelangelo's celebrated ceiling frescoes and *Giudizio universale* (Last Judgment).

Pietà (p139) A work of sculptural genius and a highlight of St Peter's Basilica.

La scuola di Atene (p145) The greatest of Raphael's frescoes, in the Vatican Museums' Stanze di Raffaello.

Amor sacro e amor profano (p157) Titian's *Sacred and Profane Love* hangs in the Museo e Galleria Borghese.

Best Baroque Beauties

Santa Teresa traffitta dall'amore di dio (p71) Chiesa di Santa Maria della Vittoria is home to this Bernini sculpture, one of the masterpieces of European baroque art.

Ratto di Proserpina (p157) Another Bernini sculpture, this one depicting Pluto abducting Proserpina, at the Museo e Galleria Borghese.

Ragazzo col canestro di frutta (p157) Admire Caravaggio's technical mastery and fearless bravado in the Museo e Galleria Borghese.

Trionfo della divina provvidenza (p71) Head to Galleria Nazionale d'Arte Antica – Palazzo Barberini for Pietro da Cortona's *Triumph of Divine Providence*.

Best Modern Art

Galleria Nazionale d'Arte Moderna (p160) Study works by futurists Giacomo Balla and Umberto Boccioni.

Museo Carlo Bilotti (p160) Boasts a collection of metaphysical paintings by maestro of the genre Giorgio de Chirico.

Museo d'Arte Contemporanea di Roma (MACRO; p161) An architectural stunner with works by Italy's post-WWII artists.

Worth a Trip

Rome's flagship contemporary art gallery is **Museo Nazionale delle Arti del XXI Secolo** (MAXXI; www.fondazionemaxxi.it; Via Guido Reni 2f; adult/reduced €11/8; 11am-7pm Tue-Fri & Sun, to 10pm Sat; Viale Tiziano). Housed in a Zaha Hadid–converted former barracks, it has a small permanent collection and hosts temporary exhibitions and installations – check the website for details.

Best
Culture

The Romans have long been passionate about culture. Ever since crowds flocked to the Colosseum for gladiatorial games, the locals have enjoyed a good show, and cultural events draw knowledgable and enthusiastic audiences. And with everything from opera to hip hop, Shakespearian drama and avant-garde installations on the program, you're sure to find a style to suit.

MAXXI BY ZAHA HADID ART ON FILE/CORBIS ©

Opera & Classical Music

Rome's abundance of beautiful settings makes it a wonderful place to catch a concert. Classical music performances – often free – are regularly held in churches, especially around Easter, Christmas and the new year, while summer sees stages set up in outdoor locations across the city. Top venues often host big-name Italian and international acts and there's a full program of gigs in the city's clubs and *centri sociali* (social centres).

Film, Drama & Exhibitions

Romans are great cinema-goers and although most films are dubbed you can still catch a movie in its original language (marked VO in listings – *versione originale*). Similarly, theatres tend to stage performances in Italian, but you might strike it lucky. You'll have no language problems enjoying the many art exhibitions that come to town.

Centri Sociali & Counterculture

Rome's alternative scene is focused on the city's *centri sociali*. These counterculture hubs, which started life as organised squats, gave rise to Italy's hip-hop and rap scenes in the 1980s and still stage alternative entertainment, be it a poetry slam, indie fashion show or a drum 'n' bass gig.

☑ **Top Tips**

▶ For listings check *Trovaroma* (a Thursday insert in *La Repubblica* newspaper).

▶ Have a look at upcoming events at www.060608. it, www.auditorium. com and www. inromenow.com.

Best for Classical Music & Opera

Auditorium Parco della Musica (p163) Rome's premier concert venue and cultural centre.

Teatro dell'Opera di Roma (p89) Rome's opera house, home to the city's opera and ballet companies.

Terme di Caracalla (p111) Haunting ancient ruins provide the spellbinding backdrop for summer opera.

Chiesa di Sant'Agnese in Agone (p44) Piazza Navona church that hosts chamber-music concerts.

Best for Jazz & Blues

Alexanderplatz (p153) Top international artists lead the way at this historic jazz club.

Big Mama (p125) Blues and jazz rule the roost at this Trastevere basement club.

Gregory's (p77) Much-loved jazz club frequented by local musicians.

Best Clubs for a Gig

Circolo degli Artisti (p93) Top Pigneto club whose headline acts have included Patti Smith and the Undertones.

Villaggio Globale (p116) A *centro sociale* that hosts gigs by emerging and cult performers.

Micca Club (p89) Eclectic club serving up everything from rockabilly festivals to burlesque performances.

Conte Staccio (p115) Catch everything from extreme electro to U2 tribute bands at this Testaccio club.

Best Exhibition Spaces

Palazzo delle Esposizioni (p85) This neoclassical cultural centre often hosts big international exhibitions.

Scuderie Papali al Quirinale (p72) A wonderful gallery housed in the pope's former stables.

MAXXI (pictured left; p183) The latest addition to Rome's contemporary arts scene; stages

avant-garde events and exhibitions.

Gagosian Gallery (p73) Organises temporary exhibitions by the big-hitters of the modern art scene.

Best Theatres

Teatro Argentina (p52) Rome's top theatre occasionally puts on performances in English.

Silvano Toti Globe Theatre (p163) Sit down to Shakespeare in Rome's faux-Elizabethan theatre.

Best for a Film

Casa del Cinema (p163) Screens indie and arthouse films and hosts movie-related events.

Nuovo Sacher (p134) Film director Nanni Moretti oversees the program at this, his personal cinema.

Worth a Trip

While the star attraction at the **Teatro Olimpico** (📞06 326 59 91; www .teatroolimpico.it; Piazza Gentile da Fabriano 17; 🚇Piazza Mancini) is the season of chamber music by the **Accademia Filarmonica Romana** (www.filarmonicaromana.org), Rome's Olympic Theatre also stages ballet, opera, occasional contemporary gigs and modern multimedia events.

Best
For Kids

Despite a reputation as a highbrow cultural destination, Rome has a lot to offer kids. Child-specific sights might be thin on the ground, but if you know where to go there's plenty to keep the little 'uns occupied. And with so much pizza and ice cream on the menu, meal times should be a breeze.

Explora – Museo dei Bambini di Roma (📞06 361 37 76; www.mdbr.it; Via Flaminia 82; adult/child over 3/child 1-3/child under 1 €7/7/3/free; ⏲entry times 10am, noon, 3pm & 5pm Tue-Sun Sep-Jul, noon, 3pm & 5pm Aug; Ⓜ Flaminio) Set up as a miniature town, this is a hands-on, feet-on, full-on museum that your nippers will love. Bookings essential at weekends.

Museo della Civiltà Romana (Piazza G Agnelli 10; adult/reduced €7.50/5.50; ⏲9am-2pm Tue-Sun; Ⓜ EUR Fermi) Out in EUR, this museum is a proven kid-pleaser, complete with a giant-scale re-creation of

4th-century Rome, detailed models of ancient buildings and weaponry, and casts of the reliefs on the Colonna di Traiano (Trajan's Column).

Palazzo Valentini (📞06 32810; www.palazzovalentini .it; Via IV Novembre 119/A; adult/child €10/free; ⏲9.30am-5.30pm Wed-Mon; 🚌Piazza Venezia) Take your older kids for a multi-media tour of the underground ruins beneath Palazzo Valentini, complete with sound effects, vividly projected frescoes and glimpses of ancient life. Book ahead, especially during holiday periods.

Bioparco (www.bioparco.it; Viale del Giardino Zoologico 1; adult/child under 12 €14/12; ⏲9.30am-6pm Apr-Oct, to 5pm Nov-Mar; 🚌Bioparco) A reliable kid-friendly choice, Rome's zoo hosts a predictable collection of animals, including lions, tigers, giraffes and monkeys, on an 18-hectare site in Villa Borghese. Children under one month old are free.

Best **Tours**

WILL SALTER/LONELY PLANET IMAGES ©

Best Walking

A Friend in Rome

(www.afriendinrome.it)
Silvia Prosperi organises private tailor-made tours (on foot, by bike or scooter) to suit your interests. She covers the Vatican and main historic centre as well as areas of interest outside the capital. Rates are €40-50 per hour, with a minimum of three hours for most tours.

Enjoy Rome (www
.enjoyrome.com; Via Marghera 8a) Offers three-hour walking tours of the Vatican (under/over 26 €27/32) and ancient and old Rome (€25/30) as well as various other walks – see the website for further details. Note that tour prices do not cover admission charges to the Vatican Museums and Colosseum.

Best by Bus

Trambus 110open (www
.trambusopen.com; family/
adult/reduced €50/20/18;
🕑 every 15min 8.30am-7pm)
This open-top, double-decker bus departs from Viale Einaudi near Termini and stops at the Colosseum, Bocca della Verità, Piazza Venezia, St Peter's, Ara Pacis and Trevi Fountain. Tickets are valid for 48 hours and allow you to hop off and on as you please.

Trambus Archeobus

(www.trambusopen.com;
family/adult €40/12;
🕑 half-hourly 9am-12.30pm & 1.20pm-4.30pm) A stop-and-go bus that runs down Via Appia Antica, stopping at points of archaeological interest along the way. It departs from Viale Einaudi near Termini and tickets are valid for 48 hours.

Best by Bike or Scooter

Bici & Baci (www.bicibaci .com; Via Cavour 302) Bici & Baci runs daily bike tours (€35) of central Rome, taking in the historic centre, Campidoglio and the Colosseum. It also offers tours on vintage Vespas and in classic Fiat 500 cars. For the Vespa and Fiat 500 tours book 24 hours ahead. Routes and prices vary according to your requests.

Best
Gay & Lesbian

Rome has a thriving, if low-key, gay scene. The big annual events, including the summer-long Gay Village, are colourful crowd-pleasers, and in 2011 Rome hosted Europride. There are relatively few queer-only venues but many of the city's top clubs host regular gay and mixed nights.

Attitudes

Rome is by nature a conservative city and its legislators have long looked to the Vatican for guidance on moral and social issues. That said, the city's gay community has taken steps out of the closet in recent years and while Rome is no San Fran on the Med, and discretion is still wise, tolerance is widespread.

Gay Village

Rome's big annual event is **Gay Village** (www.gay village.it), held between June and September in EUR (p177; although the location changes, so check ahead). Attracting up to 250,000 people and an exuberant cast of DJs, musicians and entertainers, it serves up an eclectic mix of dance music, film screenings, cultural debate and theatrical performances.

Best Gay Venues

Coming Out (p103) This popular bar is in a favourite gay area near the Colosseum.

L'Alibi (p116) On the Testaccio clubbing strip, this is an ever-popular nightclub.

Hangar (p90) Historic gay club with a relaxed vibe and a mixed clientele of locals and visitors.

ALESSANDRO07TV/SHUTTERSTOCK ©

☑ **Top Tips**

▶ Some venues ask for the Arcigay Card (€15), available on the door if required.

▶ Useful resources include **Circolo Mario Mieli di Cultura Omosessuale** (www.mariomieli.net), Rome's top gay organisation; www .gay.it (mostly in Italian); and www .nighttours.com.

Survival Guide

Survival Guide

Before You Go

When to Go

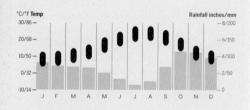

→ Winter (Dec-Feb)
Cold, short days. Museums are quiet and prices are low except at Christmas and New Year.

→ Spring (Mar-May)
Warm, sunny weather. Fervent Easter celebrations and colourful azaleas on the Spanish Steps. It's a busy time and prices are high.

→ Summer (Jun-Aug)
Very hot. Plenty of outdoor events. In August, Romans desert the city and hoteliers drop prices.

→ Autumn (Sep-Nov)
Still warm. Romaeuropa festival in town. November brings rain and low-season prices.

Book Your Stay

☑ **Top Tip** When reserving a room, ask for a *camera matrimoniale* if you want a double bed, or a *camera doppia* for twin beds.

➡ Accommodation runs the gamut from five-star palaces and designer guesthouses to family-run *pensioni* (small hotels or guesthouses), B&Bs and tranquil convents.

➡ Book in the *centro storico* (historic centre) for the best atmosphere. However, rates are high and rooms can be noisy.

➡ Other areas: Trastevere is good for party people and deep sleepers. Termini is a traveller hang-out full of hostels and budget *pensioni*; not Rome's prettiest neighbourhood. Prati is quiet and well-connected near the Vatican. Tridente is full of designer shops, boutique guesthouses and luxury five-star hotels.

➡ Standards vary but space is at a premium and rooms tend to be small, even in top-end places. Lifts are also tiny, some barely big enough to transport one person plus luggage.

➡ Noise can be a problem, so always try to get a room with double-glazed windows.

➡ Hotel rates are universally high. Most hotels offer discounts from November to March and from mid-July through August. Expect to pay top whack from April to June, September to October and at Christmas, New Year and Easter.

➡ On top of rates, Rome hotels apply a room occupancy tax. This amounts to: €2 per person per night for a maximum of 10 days in B&Bs, guesthouses and one-, two- and three-star hotels; €3 per person per night for a maximum of 10 days in four- and five-star hotels.

➡ Booking ahead is a good idea and essential during peak periods.

➡ Air-con is a sound investment, although in many cheaper places it will be turned off when you go out for the day.

Useful Websites

Bed & Breakfast Association of Rome (www.b-b.rm.it) Has B&Bs and short-term apartment rentals.

Comune di Roma (www.060608.it) Lists B&Bs, rentals and hotels (with prices).

Cross Pollinate (www.cross-pollinate.com) Has B&Bs, private apartments and guesthouses.

Lonely Planet (www.lonelyplanet.com/rome) Check author-reviewed accommodation and book online.

Santa Susanna (www.santasusanna.org/comingToRome/convents.html) A useful list of religious institutes offering accommodation.

Best Budget

Hotel Panda (www.hotelpanda.it) Long-standing favourite in the pricey Spanish Steps area.

Okapi Rooms (www.okapirooms.it) Simple, airy rooms in a townhouse near Piazza del Popolo.

Beehive (www.the-beehive.com) Boutique hostel near Termini.

La Piccola Maison (www.lapiccolamaison.com) Good-value *pensione* close to Piazza Barberini.

San Pietrino (www.sanpietrino.it) Characterful rooms in a cosy Vatican *pensione*.

Best Midrange

Arco del Lauro (www.arcodellauro.it) Minimalist comfort in medieval Trastevere.

Casa Montani (www.casamontani.com) Small, upmarket guesthouse near Piazza del Popolo.

Relais Palazzo Taverna (www.relaispalazzotaverna.com) Boutique style in the cobbled centre.

Daphne Inn (www.daphne-rome.com) Chic, modern rooms in two central locations.

Hotel Romance (www.hotelromance.it) Enjoy classic old-school comfort on the Colosseum's doorstep.

Suites Trastevere (www.trastevere.bbsuites.com) Friendly Trastevere B&B with frescoed rooms.

Best Top End

Donna Camilla Savelli (www.hotelsavelli.com) Elegant convent conversion in Trastevere.

Portrait Suites (www .portraitsuites.com) Exclusive residence owned by the Ferragamo family.

Villa Laetitia (www.villa laetitia.com) Romantic riverside villa with Fendi decor.

Villa Spalletti Trivelli (www.villaspalletti.it) Glorious mansion overlooking Quirinale gardens.

Babuino 181 (www.rome luxurysuites.com/babuino) Discreet, modern luxury on smart shopping street.

Hotel Sant'Anselmo (www.aventinohotels.com) Romantic hideaway in the graceful Aventino district.

Arriving in Rome

☑ **Top Tip** For the best way to get to your accommodation, see p17.

Aeroporto Internazionale Leonardo da Vinci (Fiumicino)

The easiest way to get from the airport is by train, but there are also bus services and private shuttle services.

Leonardo Express train (adult/child €14/free) Runs to/from Stazione Termini.

Departures from the airport every 30 minutes between 6.38am and 11.38pm, and from Termini between 5.52am and 10.52pm. Journey time is 30 minutes. Purchase tickets from vending machines in the arrivals hall and train station, and from ticket offices and *tabacchi* (newsagents).

FR1 train (one way €8) Connects the airport to Trastevere, Ostiense and Tiburtina stations, but not Termini. Departures from the airport every 15 minutes (hourly on Sunday and public holidays) between 5.58am and 11.28pm, and from Ostiense between 5.18am and 10.18pm. Purchase tickets from vending machines in the arrivals hall and train station, and from ticket offices and *tabacchi*.

Cotral bus (www.cotralspa .it; one way €5 or €7 if purchased on bus) Runs to/from Stazione Tiburtina via Stazione Termini. Eight daily departures, including night services from the airport at 1.15am, 2.15am, 3.30am and 5am, and from Tiburtina at 12.30am, 1.15am, 2.30am

and 3.45am. Journey time is one hour. Buy tickets at newsagents or tobacconists or, at the airport, from the Autogrill or Ferretti tobacconist.

SIT bus (☎06 591 68 26; www.sitbusshuttle.com; one way €6) From the airport, regular departures between 8.30am and 12.30am to Via Marsala outside Stazione Termini, and from Termini between 5am and 8.30pm. Tickets available on the bus. Journey time is one hour.

Airport Connection Services (☎06 338 32 21; www.airportconnection.it) Transfers to/from the city centre start at €27 per person.

Airport Shuttle (☎06 4201 3469; www.airportshuttle .it) Transfers to/from your hotel for €25 for one person, then €6 for each additional passenger up to a maximum of eight.

Taxi The set fare to/from the city centre is €48, which is valid for up to four passengers with luggage. Taxis registered in Fiumicino charge a set fare of €60, so make sure you catch a Comune di Roma taxi. A typical journey to the centre takes 45 to 60 minutes.

Aeroporto di Roma Ciampino

The best option is to take one of the regular bus services into the city centre. You can also take a bus to Ciampino station and then pick up a train to Stazione Termini.

Terravision bus (www .terravision.eu; one way/ return €4/8) Twice-hourly departures to/from Via Marsala outside Stazione Termini. From the airport, services are from 8.15am to 12.15am, and from Via Marsala between 4.30am and 9.20pm. Buy tickets at Terracafè in front of the Via Marsala bus stop. Journey time is 40 minutes.

SIT bus (www.sitbusshuttle .com; from airport €4, to airport €6) Regular departures from the airport to Via Marsala outside Stazione Termini between 7.45am and 11.30pm, and from Termini between 4.30am and 9.30pm. Tickets available on the bus. Journey time is 45 minutes.

Cotral bus (www.cotralspa .it; one way €3.90) Runs 17 daily services to/from

Via Giolitti near Stazione Termini. Also runs buses to/from Anagnina metro station (€1.20) and Ciampino train station (€1.20), where you can connect with services to Stazione Termini (€1.30).

Airport Connection Services (☏06 338 32 21; www.airportconnection.it) Transfers to/from the city centre start at €22 per person.

Airport Shuttle (☏06 4201 3469; www.airportshuttle .it) Transfers to/from your hotel for €25 for one person, then €5 for each additional passenger up to a maximum of eight.

Taxi The set rate between the city centre and the airport is €30. It typically takes 30 to 45 minutes.

Stazione Termini & Bus Station

Stazione Termini (Map p82, F2) is Rome's main train and transport hub, with regular services connecting to other European destinations, major Italian cities and many smaller towns.

From Termini, you can connect onto metro lines A or B, or take a bus from the bus station on Piazza

dei Cinquecento out front. Single tickets cost €1.50.

Taxis line up outside the main exit/entrance. Assume about €10 to a central Rome address.

Getting Around

Rome is a sprawling city, but the historic centre is relatively compact and it's quite possible to explore much of it on foot. The city's public transport system includes buses, trams, metro and a suburban train system. Tickets, which come in various forms, are valid on all forms of transport.

Metro

☑ **Best for...** Avoiding traffic jams and for getting around quickly.

➜ Rome's two main metro lines, line A (orange) and line B (blue), cross at Termini, the only point at which you can change from one line to the other. The much-delayed line C (green) – which will cross line A at Ottaviano and San Giovanni, and line B at Fori Imperiali Colosseo – is scheduled to open in

Tickets & Passes

Public transport tickets are valid on all modes of public transit, except on trains to Fiumicino airport.

➡ **BIT** (single ticket valid for 100 minutes and one metro ride) €1.50

➡ **BIG** (daily ticket) €6

➡ **BTI** (three-day ticket) €16.50

➡ **CIS** (weekly ticket) €24

If you intend to explore neighbourhoods beyond the historic centre (which you should), you're usually better off buying a day or multiday pass, rather than single-trip tickets.

Purchase tickets at *tabacchi* (newsagents), at news stands and from vending machines before boarding buses, trams and trains. Validate them at the metro gate or in the machines onboard buses and trams. Children under 10 travel free.

The Roma Pass (p196) comes with a three-day travel pass.

stages and be fully operational by 2018.

➡ Trains run approximately every five to 10 minutes between 5.30am and 11.30pm (to 1.30am on Friday and Saturday).

➡ All the metro stations on line B have wheelchair access except for Termini, Circo Massimo, Colosseo, Cavour (towards Laurentina) and EUR Magliana. On line A, Cipro-Musei Vaticani station is one of the few stations equipped with lifts.

➡ Take line A for the Trevi Fountain (Barberini), Spanish Steps (Spagna), and St Peter's (Ottaviano-San Pietro).

➡ Take line B for the Colosseum (Colosseo).

Bus

☑ **Best for**... Getting around the historic centre.

➡ Rome's buses and trams are run by **ATAC** (📞 06 5 70 03; www.atac .roma.it).

➡ The main bus station (Map p82, E2) is in front of Stazione Termini on Piazza dei Cinquecento, where there's an **information booth** (🕘7.30am-8pm). Other important hubs are at Largo di Torre Argentina (Map p42, C5) and Piazza Venezia (Map p30, A1).

➡ Buses generally run from about 5.30am until midnight, with limited services throughout the night.

➡ Handy routes: 64 (Termini–Centro Storico–Vatican), 40 (same route but quicker), 3 (Stazione Trastevere–Testaccio–San Giovanni–San Lorenzo–Villa Borghese) and 105 (Termini–Piazza Vittorio Emanuele II–Il Pigneto).

Night buses are marked with an N and bus stops have a blue owl symbol. Departures are usually every 15 to 30 minutes between about 1am and 5am, but can be much more infrequent. The most useful routes:

n1 Follows the route of metro line A.

n2 Follows the route of metro line B.

n7 Piazzale Clodio, Via Zanardelli, Corso Rinascimento, Corso Vittorio Emanuele II, Largo di

Torre Argentina, Piazza Venezia, Via Nazionale and Stazione Termini.

Tram

☑ **Best for**... Hopping over the river to Trastevere and for suburbs such as San Lorenzo and Il Pigneto.

The most useful tram routes for visitors:

Line 8 Connects Largo di Torre Argentina to Trastevere and beyond.

Line 2 Runs north from Piazzale Flaminio.

Line 19 Connects Il Pigneto and San Lorenzo to Quartiere Coppedè and Galleria Nazionale d'Arte Moderna.

Train

☑ **Best for**... Heading out of town to Ostia Antica.

Unless you're travelling beyond the main metropolitan area to sites such as Scavi Archeologici di Ostia Antica (p171), you shouldn't need to use Rome's suburban train network.

Taxi

☑ **Best for**... Late-night trips.

➡ Official licensed taxis are white with the symbol of Rome and an identifying number on the doors.

➡ Always go with the metered fare, never an arranged price (the set fares to and from the airports are exceptions).

➡ Flag fall is €3 between 6am and 10pm on weekdays, €4.50 on Sundays and holidays, and €6.50 between 10pm and 7am. Then it's €1.10 per kilometre. Official rates are posted in taxis.

➡ You can hail a taxi, but it's easier to wait at a rank or phone for one. There are taxi ranks at the airports, Stazione Termini (Map p82, E2), Largo di Torre Argentina (Map p42, C5), Piazza della Repubblica (Map p82, C1), Piazza del Colosseo (Map p30, D3), Piazza Belli (Map p126, D4) in Trastevere, and in the Vatican at Piazza del Pio XII (Map p148, D4) and Piazza del Risorgimento (Map p148, D3).

➡ The website www .060608.it has a list of taxi companies – click on the transport tab, then getting around by taxi.

Book by phoning the Comune di Roma's automated **taxi line** (☎06 06 09) or calling a taxi company direct. Note that the meter starts running as soon as you book.

La Capitale (☎06 49 94)

Radio Taxi (☎06 35 70)

Samarcanda (☎06 55 51)

Buses from Termini

From Piazza dei Cinquecento outside Stazione Termini, buses run to all corners of the city.

DESTINATION	BUS NO
Piazza San Pietro	40
Piazza Venezia	40/64
Piazza Navona	40/64
Campo de' Fiori	40/64
Pantheon	40/64
Colosseum	75
Terme di Caracalla	714
Villa Borghese	910
Trastevere	H

Essential Information

Business Hours

In this book, opening hours are only given when they differ from the following standards.

Banks 8.30am to 1.30pm and 2.45pm to 4.30pm Monday to Friday

Bars and cafes 7.30am to 8pm, sometimes until 1am or 2am

Shops 9am to 7.30pm or 10am to 8pm Monday to Saturday, some 11am to 7pm Sunday; smaller shops 9am to 1pm and 3.30pm to 7.30pm (or 4pm to 8pm) Monday to Saturday

Clubs 10pm to 4am

Restaurants noon to 3pm and 7.30pm to 11pm (later in summer)

Discount Cards

☑ **Top Tip** If you use the Roma Pass for more expensive sights such as the Capitoline Museums, it's real value for money.

➡ Discount cards can be purchased at any of the museums and monuments listed below. The Roma Pass is also available at tourist information kiosks.

➡ EU citizens aged between 18 and 25 qualify for a discount at most galleries and museums. Under 18s and over 65s often get in free. In both cases you'll need proof of age, ideally a passport or ID card.

Archaeologia Card (adult/reduced €24/14.50) Valid seven days. Gives entrance to the Colosseum, Roman Forum, Palatino, Terme di Caracalla, Museo Nazionale Romano, Mausoleo di Cecilia Metella and Villa dei Quintili.

Roma Pass (www.romapass.it; €34) Valid three days. Includes free admission to two museums or archaeological sites, reduced entry to extra sites and events, and unlimited public transport within Rome.

Electricity

230V/50Hz

230V/50Hz

Emergency

Ambulance (☎118)

Fire (☎115)

Police (☎113 or ☎112)

Money

☑ **Top Tip** The daily cash withdrawal limit at ATMs is €250.

Italy uses the euro. Euro notes come in denominations of €500, €200, €100, €50, €20, €10 and €5; coins come in denominations of €2 and €1, and 50, 20, 10, five, two and one cents.

Admission Prices

➡ In this book we give adult and reduced admission prices.

➡ Reduced admission is typically for EU citizens between 18 and 24, or, in some cases, for EU residents between six and 25 and over 65.

ATMs

➡ ATMs (known as *bancomat*) are widely available and most will accept cards tied to the Visa, MasterCard, Cirrus and Maestro systems.

➡ Always let your bank know when you're going abroad, in case they block your card when payments appear from unusual locations.

Credit Cards

➡ Virtually all midrange and top-end hotels accept credit cards, as do most restaurants and large shops. Some cheaper *pensioni*, trattorias and pizzerias only accept cash. Don't rely on credit cards at museums or galleries.

➡ Major cards such as Visa, MasterCard, Eurocard, Cirrus and Eurocheques are widely accepted. Amex is also recognised, although it's less common than Visa or MasterCard.

In case of emergency, you can call the following numbers to have your card blocked:

Amex (☎06 7290 0347)

Diners Club (☎800 393939)

MasterCard (☎800 870866)

Visa (☎800 819014)

Money Changers

➡ There are exchange booths at Stazione Termini and at Fiumicino and Ciampino airports.

➡ Take your passport, or photo ID, when exchanging money.

Tipping

If service (*servizio*) is not included, leave a euro or two in pizzerias, 10% in restaurants. Rounding your taxi fare to the nearest euro will suffice.

Money-Saving Tips

➡ Visit the Vatican Museums on the last Sunday of the month – they're free.

➡ Check for cultural initiatives that give free admission to museums, galleries and archaeological sites.

➡ Look out for free concerts during festivals.

➡ Fill up on art at Rome's churches – they're all free.

➡ Buy a Roma Pass if you want to blitz the sights.

➡ Lunch on pizza slices and ice cream; dine on bar snacks over an *aperitivo* (aperitif).

➡ Drink coffee standing at the bar rather than sitting at a table.

Tip porters about €4 at A-list hotels.

Public Holidays

Capodanno (New Year's Day) 1 January

Epifania (Epiphany) 6 January

Pasquetta (Easter Monday) March/April

Giorno della Liberazione (Liberation Day) 25 April

Festa del Lavoro (Labour Day) 1 May

Festa della Repubblica (Republic Day) 2 June

Festa dei Santi Pietro e Paolo (Feast of St Peter & St Paul) 29 June

Ferragosto (Feast of the Assumption) 15 August

Festa di Ognisanti (All Saints' Day) 1 November

Festa dell'Immacolata Concezione (Feast of the Immaculate Conception) 8 December

Natale (Christmas Day) 25 December

Festa di Santo Stefano (Boxing Day) 26 December

Safe Travel

☑ **Top Tip** Pickpockets go where the tourists go.

Rome is not a dangerous city, but petty theft is a problem. Watch out for pickpockets around the Colosseum, Piazza di Spagna, Piazza San Pietro, Stazione Termini and on crowded public transport – the 64 Vatican bus is notorious.

To minimise risks:

➡ Keep essentials in a money belt but carry your day's spending money in a separate wallet.

➡ Wear your bag/camera strap across your body and away from the road – thieves on scooters can swipe a bag and be gone in seconds.

➡ Never drape your bag over an empty chair at a street-side cafe or put it where you can't see it.

➡ Always check your change to see you haven't been short-changed.

In case of theft or loss, report the incident to the police within 24 hours and ask for a statement.

Telephone

Mobile Phones

Italy uses the GSM 900/1800 cellular system, compatible with phones from the UK, Europe, Australia and most of Asia, and dual-band GSM 1900/900 phones from North America and Japan.

You can buy a prepaid (*prepagato*) SIM card from **TIM** (www.tim.it), **Wind** (www.wind.it) or **Vodafone** (www.vodafone.it) outlets across town.

Italian mobile-phone numbers are nine or 10 digits and begin with a three-digit prefix starting with 3.

Country & City Codes

Italy's country code is ☎39, and the Rome area code is ☎06. Don't omit the 0 if calling Rome from abroad. To call abroad from Italy, dial ☎00 before the country code.

Toilets

☑ **Top Tip** If there are no public toilets nearby, nip into a bar.

There are toilets at the Colosseum, Piazza San Pietro, Castel Sant'Angelo and Stazione Termini (€1).

Tourist Information

There are information points at **Fiumicino** (Terminal 3, International Arrivals; ◷8am-7.30pm) and **Ciampino** (International Arrivals, baggage reclaim area; ◷9am-6.30pm) airports. Also at the following locations across the city, open 9.30am to 7pm (except at Termini):

Castel Sant'Angelo (Map p148, F4; Piazza Pia)

Piazza Navona (Map p42, B2) Near Piazza delle Cinque Lune.

Via dei Fori Imperiali (Map p32, C2)

Stazione Termini (Map p82, F3; ⊙8am-7.30pm) Next to platform 24.

Trevi Fountain (Map p70, A4; Via Marco Minghetti) Closer to Via del Corso than the fountain.

Via Nazionale (Map p82, A2)

For Vatican information there's the **Centro Servizi Pellegrini e Turisti** (Map p148, C4; ☎06 6988 1662; Piazza San Pietro; ⊙8.30am-6pm Mon-Sat).

Phone and internet resources include the following:

060608 (☎06 06 08; www.060608.it; ⊙9am-9pm) Provides information on shows, hotels, transport etc; you can also book theatre, concert, exhibition and museum tickets.

Turismo Roma (www .turismoroma.it) Rome's official tourist site has accommodation and restaurant lists, as well as details of upcoming events, museums and much more.

Dos & Don'ts

Do...

➡ Greet people with a *buongiorno* (good morning) or *buonasera* (good evening).

➡ Dress the part – cover up when visiting churches and go smart when eating out.

➡ Eat pasta with a fork not a spoon, and keep your hands on the table not under it.

Don't...

➡ Feel you have to order everything on the menu. No one seriously expects you to eat a starter, pasta, second course and dessert.

➡ Order cappuccino after lunch or dinner. Well, OK, you can, but Romans don't.

➡ Wait for cars to stop at pedestrian crossings. You'll have to make the first move if you want to cross the road.

Travellers with Disabilities

☑ **Top Tip** Metro line A is pretty much off-limits to wheelchairs, but bus 590 follows the same route.

➡ Cobbled streets, blocked pavements and tiny lifts make Rome a difficult city for travellers with disabilities.

➡ On metro line B all stations have wheelchair access except for Termini, Circo Massimo, Colosseo, Cavour and EUR Magliana.

➡ Check out www.handy turismo.it, which has information on travel, accommodation and access at the main tourist attractions.

Visas

EU citizens do not need a visa for Italy. Nationals of Australia, Canada, Israel, Japan, New Zealand, Switzerland and the USA do not need a visa for stays of up to 90 days.

Italy is one of the 15 signatories of the Schengen Convention. The standard tourist visa for a Schengen country is valid for 90 days. You must apply for it in your country of residence.

Language

Regional dialects are an important part of identity in many parts of Italy, but you'll have no trouble being understood in Rome or anywhere else in the country if you stick to standard Italian, which is what we've also used in this chapter.

The sounds used in spoken Italian can all be found in English. If you read our pronunciation guides as if they were English, you'll be understood. The stressed syllables are indicated with italics. Note that *ai* is pronounced as in 'aisle', *ay* as in 'say', *ow* as in 'how', *dz* as the 'ds' in 'lids', and that *r* is a strong and rolled sound.

To enhance your trip with a phrase-book, visit **lonelyplanet.com**. Lonely Planet iPhone phrasebooks are available through the Apple App store.

Basics

Hello.
Buongiorno. bwon·*jor*·no

Goodbye.
Arrivederci. a·ree·ve·*der*·chee

How are you?
Come sta? *ko*·me sta

Fine. And you?
Bene. E Lei? *be*·ne e lay

Please.
Per favore. per fa·*vo*·re

Thank you.
Grazie. *gra*·tsye

Excuse me.
Mi scusi. mee *skoo*·zee

Sorry.
Mi dispiace. mee dees·*pya*·che

Yes./No.
Sì./No. see/no

I don't understand.
Non capisco. non ka·*pee*·sko

Do you speak English?
Parla inglese? *par*·la een·*gle*·ze

Eating & Drinking

I'd like ...	*Vorrei ...*	vo·*ray* ...
a coffee	*un caffè*	oon ka·*fe*
a table	*un tavolo*	oon ta·*vo*·lo
the menu	*il menù*	eel me·*noo*
two beers	*due birre*	*doo*·e *bee*·re

What would you recommend?
Cosa mi consiglia? *ko*·za mee kon·*see*·lya

Enjoy the meal!
Buon appetito! bwon a·pe·*tee*·to

That was delicious!
Era squisito! *e*·ra skwee·*zee*·to

Cheers!
Salute! sa·*loo*·te

Can you bring me the bill, please?
Mi porta il conto, per favore? mee *por*·ta eel *kon*·to per fa·*vo*·re

Shopping

I'd like to buy ...
Vorrei comprare ... vo·*ray* kom·*pra*·re ...

I'm just looking.
Sto solo guardando. sto *so*·lo gwar·*dan*·do

How much is this?
Quanto costa   kwan·to kos·ta
questo?   kwe·sto

It's too expensive.
È troppo caro/   e tro·po ka·ro/
cara. (m/f)   ka·ra

Emergencies

Help!
Aiuto!   a·yoo·to

Call the police!
Chiami la   kya·mee la
polizia!   po·lee·tsee·a

Call a doctor!
Chiami un   kya·mee oon
medico!   me·dee·ko

I'm sick.
Mi sento male.   mee sen·to ma·le

I'm lost.
Mi sono perso/   mee so·no per·so/
persa. (m/f)   per·sa

Where are the toilets?
Dove sono i   do·ve so·no ee
gabinetti?   ga·bee·ne·tee

Time & Numbers

What time is it?
Che ora è?   ke o·ra e

It's (two) o'clock.
Sono le (due).   so·no le (doo·e)

morning	*mattina*	ma·tee·na
afternoon	*pomeriggio*	po·me·ree·jo
evening	*sera*	se·ra
yesterday	*ieri*	ye·ree
today	*oggi*	o·jee
tomorrow	*domani*	do·ma·nee

1	*uno*	oo·no
2	*due*	doo·e
3	*tre*	tre
4	*quattro*	kwa·tro
5	*cinque*	cheen·kwe
6	*sei*	say
7	*sette*	se·te
8	*otto*	o·to
9	*nove*	no·ve
10	*dieci*	dye·chee
100	*cento*	chen·to
1000	*mille*	mee·le

Transport & Directions

Where's ...?
Dov'è ...?   do·ve ...

What's the address?
Qual'è   kwa·le
l'indirizzo?   leen·dee·ree·tso

Can you show me (on the map)?
Può mostrarmi   pwo mos·trar·mee
(sulla pianta)? (soo·la pyan·ta)

At what time does the ... leave?
A che ora   a ke o·ra
parte ...?   par·te ...

Does it stop at ...?
Si ferma a ...? see fer·ma a ...

How do I get there?
Come ci si   ko·me chee see
arriva?   a·ree·va

bus	*autobus*	ow·to·boos
ticket	*biglietto*	bee·lye·to
timetable	*orario*	o·ra·ryo
train	*il treno*	eel tre·no

Beh/ind the Scenes

Send Us Your Feedback

We love to hear from travellers – your comments help make our books better. We read every word, and we guarantee that your feedback goes straight to the authors. Visit **lonelyplanet.com/contact** to submit your updates and suggestions.

Note: We may edit, reproduce and incorporate your comments in Lonely Planet products such as guidebooks, websites and digital products, so let us know if you don't want your comments reproduced or your name acknowledged. For a copy of our privacy policy visit lonelyplanet.com/privacy.

Our Readers

Many thanks to the travellers who used the last edition and wrote to us with helpful hints, useful advice and interesting anecdotes:

Liz Edinburgh, Stefan Konarski, Peter E Presford

Duncan's Thanks

Thanks to Joe Bindloss for the commission and his help and support on the job. As always, *grazie mille* to Lidia and the boys, Ben and Nick, for putting up with my long absences during research and the days spent at my computer writing it all up.

Acknowledgments

Cover photograph: St Peter's Basilica, Jean-Pierre Lescourret/Getty. Many of the images in this guide are available for licensing from Lonely Planet Images: www.lonelyplanetimages.com.

This Book

This 3rd edition of Lonely Planet's *Pocket Rome* guidebook was researched and written by Duncan Garwood. The previous two editions were written by Cristian Bonetto. This guidebook was commissioned in Lonely Planet's London office, and produced by the following:

Commissioning Editor Joe Bindloss **Coordinating Editors** Carolyn Boicos, Monique Perrin **Coordinating Cartographer** Csanad Csutoros **Coordinating Layout Designer** Clara Monitto **Managing Editors** Anna Metcalfe, Martine Power **Senior Editors** Andi Jones, Susan Paterson **Managing Cartographers** Amanda Sierp, Diana Von

Holdt **Managing Layout Designer** Jane Hart **Cover Research** Naomi Parker **Internal Image Research** Nicholas Colicchia **Language Content** Samantha Forge, Annelies Mertens **Thanks to** Ryan Evans, Larissa Frost, Chris Girdler, Wayne Murphy, Trent Paton, Anthony Phelan, Laura Stansfeld, Gerard Walker, Dora Whitaker

Index

See also separate subindexes for:

⊗ Eating p206
🍷 Drinking p207
✪ Entertainment p207
🛍 Shopping p207

Augustus, Emperor 34, 59
Aurelian Wall 106
Aventino & Testaccio 108-17, **110**
  drinking 115
  entertainment 115-16
  food 112-15
  itineraries 109
  shopping 116-17
  sights 111-12
  transport 109

Sights p000
Map Pages **p000**